The Raw Truth

The Raw Truth

The Art of Preparing Living Foods

by Jeremy A. Safron

CELESTIAL ARTS

Berkeley / Toronto

This book is dedicated to all living things. Especially to those who believe.

CA

Celestial Arts
P.O. Box 7123
Berkeley, California 94707
www.tenspeed.com

Distributed in Australia by Simon and Schuster Australia, in Canada by Ten Speed Press Canada, in New Zealand by Southern Publishers Group, in South Africa by Real Books, in Southeast Asia by Berkeley Books, and in the United Kingdom and Europe by Airlift Book Company.

Cover illustration by Karina Blu
Cover design by Chloe Nelson
Text design by Betsy Stromberg and Chloe Nelson

Library of Congress Cataloging-in-Publication Data
Safron, Jeremy, 1971–
    The raw truth : the art of preparing living foods / Jeremy Safron.
      p. cm.
    ISBN 1-58761-172-4 (pbk.)
    1. Cookery (Natural foods) 2. Raw foods. I. Title.
  TX741.S24 2003
  641.5'63—dc21   2002155699

First printing, 2003
Printed in Canada

1 2 3 4 5 6 7 8 9 10 — 08 07 06 05 04 03

Contents

Introduction

With the correct tools and the proper resources, we can accomplish anything we wish. Experience (what we do) plus knowledge (what we learn) gives us wisdom (what we can share).

Raw Experience

Experience is the greatest teacher there is. Our lives are our lessons and contained within them is the information that will allow us to grow. It is up to each individual to decide and choose what their life will hold. Each lesson we learn leads to the next one, and as we encounter greater diversity our ability to comprehend increases. There are many choices that we have the opportunity to make, and these choices help define how we relate to our world. We change our world as much as our world changes us. The less impact we create upon this world the more of it we will be able to enjoy in our future. Reading or hearing about the experience of others is not the same as experiencing something ourselves. We may understand someone else's experience, learning from it is a different matter. The more positive our experiences, the more positive we become about our lives. Savor each experience, for they all help to make us who we are.

Raw Knowledge

The basis of raw foodism is that life promotes life. Food fresh from nature's garden contains a wide range of nutrients and a powerful amount of life force. Raw foodists believe in living as closely to the earth as possible and respecting all life. We suggest growing your own food and trading with other farmers or obtaining it from local farmers' markets or even foraging for it. We advocate the use of food as medicine, and fasting as a way to cleanse and purify your body and soul. We recognize that if you feed a person a sprout they eat for a day, but if you teach them to sprout, they eat for life and can teach others, too. With the correct tools and the proper resources, we can accomplish anything we choose.

Foods that have been heated or overly processed have lost most (usually all) of their life force. The beneficial enzyme content of a food is completely destroyed by the act of heating, causing the digestive system and body to work much harder to gain any energy or nutrition. If we heated a human body to over 108°F, it would be very uncomfortable, and if we went over 116°F, it would be dead. The same can be said of our foods.

Another tenet of raw foodism is the idea that eating to live is better than living to eat. Most of what is consumed today is overly processed. It has been commercialized to the point of being poison. In fact, much of the food eaten today is "edible media"; mainstream society eats for entertainment rather than energy and nutrition. This edible media usually contains little to no nutrition or life force. It is well packaged and marketed so people continue to eat it.

Many people have thought they could outsmart nature and profit by isolating the substance in a food that was beneficial. At first people ate oranges and were healthy. Then someone discovered vitamin C and felt it was the healthful part of the orange. Later it was realized that ascorbic acid was important for absorption of the vitamin C. Then they figured out that it was the bioflavonoids they needed. Eventually, they will realize that all we needed was the orange all along and that nature had made it perfect in the first place.

There are all sorts of different ideas within the world of raw food. Some people consider raw foods to be just fruits and leaves, while others suggest dining on elaborate raw recipes made in the tradition of a variety of cultures. There are groups who only eat living food—foods that may have been cooked at one point but have been fully digested by a living culture like miso or nama shoyu. Sproutarians eat mostly sprouts and fruitarians eat only fruits.

Personally, I eat very little now after eating only raw foods for nearly ten years. I dry fast until noon or later, then eat wheatgrass or a coconut. During the afternoon, I drink juice or smoothies or eat coconuts or other whole fruits. In the evenings, I eat whole fruits and one day a week I prepare and eat an elaborate raw meal. Additionally, one day a week I fast on water or coconuts. I eat lots of fresh vital foods picked wild in the jungles and forests and forage or grow almost 80 percent of my food. My current philosophy is bio-unity—being one with nature and foraging or gardening as much as possible of the foods I eat and always being creative and loving with food.

My suggestion for people transitioning to a raw lifestyle is "take the best and leave the rest." Find the raw-food philosophy or style that works with your life. Whether it is starting the day raw and going as long as you can, or taking one day a week to eat only raw food, be sure to transition in a comfortable way. Going raw can be very easy for some and more challenging for others . . . just like becoming vegetarian. It is a matter of making a conscious decision to eat from the plant kingdom and then educating yourself properly in order to maintain a high level of health.

Eating involves intent as well as nutrition and life force. When we eat foods made with love, we are inspired; when we eat food made with anger we get upset. The way food is handled and cared for also affects its general energy. Food is sensitive to energy: intent and action either help keep the food pure or corrupt it. Grandma's soup doesn't heal because it's soup or because of the recipe—it's Grandma's love that heals. A romantic dinner isn't romantic because of the ingredients, it's the love that makes it what it is. These examples help demonstrate how our intent and thoughts can affect our food. This is true for life as well as food. If we enter into a situation with positive intent, we can do anything, and if we act with negativity, anger, fear, and worry, we just can't seem to do anything right. Remember that your words and thoughts make up your world and that our bodies and lives are a reflection of our mind's experience of itself. We are what we think: positive, loving intentions create positive experiences. Intention is everything.

Raw Wisdom

The world always needs heroes and champions. Whether it has been Robin Hood, da Vinci, Bruce Lee, or Abe Lincoln, the world has always had people promoting new ideas and standing forth for the cause of liberation. The heroes of today champion the causes of natural health and evolved consciousness.

My own raw experience began in 1993, when I decided to create a company dedicated to the promotion of raw food. At the time there were very few people teaching about the subject and even fewer resources for raw foodists. I started a company called Loving Foods, in upstate New York, with the purpose of educating people about raw food and providing delicious-tasting meals to help show that raw food wasn't just nuts and salads. Our response from the community was great and the company grew. The catering jobs rolled in, and I began to write a book called *The Raw Truth* that would eventually become the book you are reading today.

My journey with raw foods continued when I traveled on to Hawaii, where I was the head chef at a retreat center. The people in town found out there was someone making awesome raw food at the center and they started sneaking in for dinner. One night the manager of the spa asked why there were forty people eating, when the center's current workshop only had twenty people enrolled.

It was at that point that I realized I needed a restaurant. In 1996 I opened the Raw Experience in Paia, on Maui. From day one the restaurant was a success. People from all over the world came to eat the amazing creations made by my staff of highly trained and well-focused chefs. As the restaurant's popularity grew, I evolved *The Raw Truth* into a recipe book and self-published it in late 1996. I was amazed at the response (there were almost no raw-food books available at the time). Since then, we have invented many more fabulous recipes (some of those you'll find here, in this new edition) and inspired many people to try raw foods.

The restaurant was thriving and I began to travel the world educating people, helping open other raw-food restaurants, and training chefs. I also began teaching yoga, meditation, kung fu, chi kung, and mental evolution. As I blossomed as a teacher I began to counsel people, helping them find their own power as I had found mine. I continue to study as well as teach and travel, always holding space for the future of natural living.

The tools, techniques, and recipes you'll find on the following pages will give you a solid understanding of raw living. Use the knowledge to inspire or enhance your own raw experience.

Raw Facts

The advantages to eating raw food include everything from ingesting food containing live enzymes to consuming food with higher vitamin content and other vital life-force nutrients. Heat changes the makeup of all things. When food is heated, it is chemically altered and loses most of its ability to provide energy. Eating raw food provides 100 percent of the nutrition available to us. According to Dr. Ann Wigmore of the Ann Wigmore Natural Health Institute, the same food in cooked form can have up to 85 percent less nutritional value. Once cooked, many foods combine together to form new substances that may be palatable, but are by no means beneficial.

Eating living foods also helps us obtain all of its enzymes, catalysts which help us digest our food. Enzymes remain intact within living foods below temperatures of 116°F (ideally 108°F); higher temperatures destroy the enzymes and our bodies have to work harder to digest the foods we consume. Enzyme-rich foods help provide our bodies with a more viable and efficient energy source. Raw foods rapidly digest in our stomach and begin to provide energy and nutrition at a quick rate. When you consume cooked food, either alone or before raw food, it can cause a condition called leukocytosis, an increase in white blood cells. Our bodies may respond to cooked food as if it were a foreign bacteria or a diseased cell, which causes our immune system to waste energy on defending us. By eating only raw food or eating raw food before cooked food, you can prevent leukocytosis.

Raw food contains all the necessary enzymes to break itself down, thereby providing you with the maximum amount of energy with minimal bodily effort.

Raw food is in its original form and therefore more wholesome, assimilable, and digestible. Food eaten raw creates very little impact on the body's systems. I find that raw food provides a far greater range of taste then when eaten cooked. Animals have been eating raw food since time began. Plants take Earth's natural resources and produce a substance that provides energy without a need for alteration. It is truly a gift to be respectful and gentle with the diversity of foods that nature provides, in the process benefiting both ourselves and the natural world we live in.

A Plant's Intention

A plant's intention is to grow. It sprouts from a seed and produces and uses chlorophyll to combine sunlight and carbon dioxide with other nutrients found in soil to create more of itself. As more and more leaves are produced, a plant matures enough to bear fruit. Plants take the elemental minerals in soil (in their raw form), absorb them, and transform them into organic minerals that animals can assimilate. Plants are not harmed when their fruit is eaten. It actually benefits the plant. The fruit's intention is to be eaten so that its seeds can spread to other places to further propagate the species. To enable this process, fruit looks and tastes delicious. In many ways all creatures who eat fruit are giving life to future generations of fruit, as well as absorbing nutrients. Some plants continually produce fruit, while others produce fruit once and pass back into the earth. Plant a seed and create a future meal: As we sow, so shall we reap.

Preprogrammed versus Processed

In today's world food, commercially produced foods are grown with a program. First, a seed is planted. For the most part this seed is not planted with the intention to forward life, but rather to benefit the farmer financially. Then, the seeds grow to plants and are often treated with toxic chemicals (under the guise of protecting the plants and us from bugs). After that, the plants are either harvested by fossil fuel–burning machines or by poorly paid, disgruntled workers. The fruits and vegetables produced from these plants are then shipped, usually many miles, and tossed and thrown around by workers who care nothing for the produce.

Often the next step is that the fruits and vegetables are put on a shelf by an underpaid produce clerk where they get sprayed down with chlorinated water (after they have been coated with animal-based wax. This produce is often made to look homogenous, and it tastes like a synthetic version of fruits and vegetables. In the store the fruits and vegetables sit under fluorescent lights until someone buys them and takes them home. Sometimes the produce is sent to factories, where machines with grease and dirt flying about mash, mutilate, cook, and kill every possible raw nutrient and all life force. Then the fruits and vegetables are packaged and sent to a supermarket near you where they sit on the shelf indefinitely. By the time you buy the box or can containing the fruits and vegetables, there may be more nutritional value in the box then in the product inside.

From the Tree Right to Me

Conversely, there are still some farmers who refuse to participate in the mass mechanization and chemicalization of the food industry. They grow their food without chemicals or pesticides and still harvest by hand. This food is referred to as "organic" or "unsprayed," and from a nutritional and energetic point of view it is the best store-bought food to consume. There are many alternatives to commercial mass-produced food. Local farmers' markets, farmstands, co-ops, and natural food stores offer an abundance of consciously raised, organic, unsprayed, and locally grown food. Homegrown foods and those harvested from the wild are the best available. Only nature and the forager are involved in creating a direct connection between the earth and human. Growing your own food in a greenhouse or garden is a way to ensure that love goes into the growth of a plant. When we interact with our food in a positive way, the food provides far more energy. Positive interaction with plants can increase the plant's yield and vitality.

Chlorophyll

Chlorophyll is liquid life. All plant life is based upon it. Plants use chlorophyll in photosynthesis to transform sunlight and carbon dioxide into sugar and oxygen. The chlorophyll cell and the human red blood cell are molecularly almost identical. When ingested, chlorophyll is almost instantly absorbed into the body and feeds abundant amounts of oxygen to the blood, brain, and other organs, allowing them to function at an optimal level.

Chlorophyll creates an unfriendly environment for harmful bacteria, helping to protect the body from virus and infection. It helps build the immune system, detoxifies the organs and cells of the body, cleanses the liver of accumulated toxic oils, and aids in healing wounds. Chlorophyll helps protect cells from the harmful effects of radiation from electric substations, televisions, computers, X rays, nuclear power plants, and nuclear waste. Chlorophyll can be found in all green plants. Some plants, such as wheatgrass, are made up of as much as 70 percent chlorophyll and can help heal wounds extremely fast. The production of chlorophyll begins with sprouting seeds, which use light and water to create life. Chlorophyll-rich food is high in vital enzymes and rich in B vitamins. Chlorophyll also increases cell growth and thereby helps the body regenerate. Young grasses and sprouts are some of the best sources of chlorophyll. Chlorophyll is destroyed by heat. A temperature of greater than 108°F begins to break down the chlorophyll in plants. The greater the temperature, the faster the chlorophyll is destroyed. Therefore, food rich in chlorophyll should be eaten raw and not cooked.

Enzymes

Live enzymes are essential to digestion. Enzymes break down the food we eat into a usable form for the body. When a food is exposed to temperatures greater than 116°F (108°F to be safe), most of its enzymes are killed. Enzyme-depleted food can be very hard to digest and gives very little energy to the body. Without the valuable enzymes contained in raw and living food, our body must produce some of its own enzymes to digest food. This process leaves the body drained of energy. Raw and living food can fill the body with energy and vibrancy rapidly by breaking down food quickly for easy digestion and assimilation. Since many nuts and seeds contain a coating of enzyme inhibitors that stop the digestion or breakdown of the seed, seeds should be soaked in water or sprouted so they become digestible, alive, and nutrient packed.

Assimilation and Elimination

Illnesses or diseases are symptoms of either poor assimilation or poor elimination. For many reasons, from deficient diet to poor lifestyle choices, the body can become filled with toxic matter that poisons the body, mind, and spirit. This toxic matter sometimes clogs the body and greatly reduces the ability of the body to absorb nutrients. The body then becomes starved of valuable vitamins, minerals, and amino acids that keep the body functioning optimally. This is known as poor assimilation.

When toxic or harmful substances are taken into the body but cannot be moved out of the body, it is called poor elimination. Organic raw and living food benefits both assimilation and elimination, helping to keep the body free from illness.

Organically Distilled Water

Water is one of the fundamental elements of life. We humans are made up of almost 80 percent water. Finding pure sources of water is of the utmost importance in this modern era when environmental toxins abound. In ancient times, the purest water came from wells, streams, and rainwater. Now, after a hundred years of high usage of chemicals and pesticides, well water, rivers, and rain are often polluted. Tap water is even worse as it's usually been treated with "cleansing" chemicals. Additionally, tap water along with bottled water often goes through plastic pipes (a synthetic material, neither organic nor inorganic). There are various methods of obtaining pure water through mechanical or natural means—such as evaporation or filtration—but the best source of all is directly from plants.

Plants have the natural ability to distill water. A tree will draw inorganic minerals into its roots from stream runoff, rain, and underground springs and transform it into organically distilled water that it will store in its leaves and fruits. Water held in the plant's living cells is organically distilled water and can be obtained by juicing or eating watery fruits or by drinking coconut water. The method by which modern water purifiers remove unwanted chemicals and bacteria is very similar to that of a plant. Filters range from filtering out only odor and taste to removing all unwanted inorganic minerals and harmful bacteria. Reverse osmosis systems are some of the highest quality home filters available. Many people in the natural hygiene tradition use water distillers, which evaporate the water and recondense it leaving toxic sediment behind. There are also companies that sell bottled water that is especially pure and water that has been ozonated or oxygenated.

Both filtered water and organically distilled water can be further improved through a restructuring process resulting in what's referred to as *charged water*. To make charged water, pour purified or clean water back and forth three to seven times between two glass jars, then leave it to settle in one of the jars. Add a quartz crystal to the water, then put the water in direct sunlight for twenty-four hours or more. The resulting water will be recharged and holistically structured.

The Four Living Food Groups

The four primary categories of living foods are fresh food, sprouted food, cultured food, and dehydrated food.

Fresh food is any type of raw food that is ready for use in its vibrant unadulterated form. Examples of fresh food are fruits, vegetables, fresh herbs, and other harvested food. It is very important to consume large amounts of fresh food. These should make up 50 percent to 70 percent of your daily intake of food. Fresh food contains a high amount of organically distilled water (up to 85 percent). Fresh food also contains many vital nutrients and is rich in vitamins. There is a wide variety of fresh food and, when possible, it is best to eat fresh produce grown in your own area. Fresh foods represent the element of Water and are life giving.

Sprouted food is any type of seed, nut, grain, or bean that has been soaked in water, exposed to air and indirect sunlight, and, when rinsed daily, forms a new plant, beginning with a sprout. Some examples are almond sprouts, buckwheat sprouts, sunflower sprouts, and mung bean sprouts. Sprouted food is often very high in chlorophyll. In many plants the highest levels of chlorophyll exist while the plant is in its youngest and most vital stages. Sprouted food is very helpful in the building of new cells, provides existing cells with additional oxygen, and helps rejuvenate the body. Sprouted foods represent the element of Air and are regenerating and cleansing.

Cultured food is any type of food that has had a beneficial culture introduced into it (acidophilus, koji, and bifidus, for example). These cultures then grow and proliferate within the food. Some examples are miso, amazake, seed cheeze, kim chee, and tofu. Fermented and cultured foods help to promote healthy bacteria within the digestive system. These "friendly" bacteria help break down our food and hand us the vital nutrients that we need. Higher concentrations of good bacteria in our digestive system allows for both faster and more efficient absorption of food. A strong concentration of friendly bacteria also maintains a healthy balance within the intestines that does not leave room for unfriendly bacteria such as *E. coli* and candida to grow. Cultured foods represent the element of Fire and are energizing and transformational.

Dehydrated food is any type of food that has had the water removed from it through gentle drying at low heat levels. Some examples are dried fruits, Essene bread, and dried herbs. Foods that have had the water removed from them are very concentrated. By removing the water and decreasing the mass of the food, dehydrated food allows the intake of greater quantities of nutrients and leaves an intensified version of the food. Dehydrated food is considered alive only when dried at or below 108°F (the point at which enzymes die and other vitamins and minerals break down). Most dried food retains its nutrients longer because it's unaffected by the breakdown caused by water trapped within the cells. Dried food can also be rehydrated. Dehydrated foods represent the element of Earth and are very grounding and sustaining.

BIO-DESTRUCTIVE TO BIO-GENIC FOODS

Bio-Destructive (Food that is hurtful.)
Bio-destructive foods damage and destroy the body's organs and cells and deplete the body's ability to heal itself. These foods are toxic.

Chemicals
Preservatives
Hormone-raised animal products
Synthetic materials
Food cooked in aluminum
Artificial colors and flavors

Bio-Degenerative (Food that is harmful.)
Bio-degenerative foods have a destructive effect over time.
They weaken the body and can eventually cause disease.

Meats
Overcooked and packaged food
Old and rotting food
Canned food
Inorganic materials
Processed food
Cooked oils
Foods frozen for too long
Homogenized and industrially produced dairy products
Unknown and unpronounceable substances
Food made with anger

Bio-Static (Food that is inert.)

Bio-static foods require time and energy to digest, giving very little (if anything at all) back to the body. These foods may slightly sustain life.

Cooked fruits
Cooked vegetables
Cooked grains
Cooked beans
Frozen foods
Foods dried at high temperatures

Bio-Active (Food that is helpful.)

Bio-active foods have many vital nutrients and allow the body to function optimally. These foods build and maintain the body's normal processes.

Raw, live, organic food
Whole food
Amino-rich food
Enzyme-rich food
Food dried at low temperatures

Bio-Regenerative or Bio-Genic (Food that heals.)

Bio-genic foods repair the body and promote longevity and healing.

Rejuvenating food
Sprouts and chlorophyll-rich food
Cultured food
Medicinal herbs
Fresh, wild, hand-picked food
Food made with love

LOVING FOODS: FOUR LIVING FOOD GROUPS

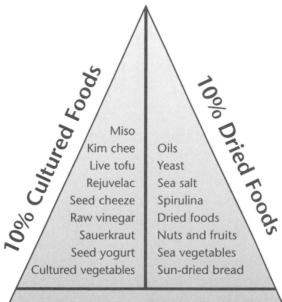

10% Cultured Foods

Miso
Kim chee
Live tofu
Rejuvelac
Seed cheeze
Raw vinegar
Sauerkraut
Seed yogurt
Cultured vegetables

10% Dried Foods

Oils
Yeast
Sea salt
Spirulina
Dried foods
Nuts and fruits
Sea vegetables
Sun-dried bread

20% Sprouted Foods*

Alfalfa   Clover   Wheat   Corn   Oat   Rye
Wild rice   Millet   Quinoa   Amaranth   Onion
Garlic   Pumpkin   Barley   Almond   Sesame
Sunflower   Garbanzo   Soy   Lentil   Pea   Hazelnut

*All seeds, nuts, and beans are sproutable; some grow sprouts, some grow greens, and some grow grasses.

60% Fresh Foods*

Juicy fruits   Berries   Sweet fruits   Fresh nuts   Juices   Curcubits
Nightshades   Greens   Wild herbs   Roots   Allium   Brassica
Mushrooms   Flowers

* Unheated (raw), organic foods from nature.

Raw Foods

Finding pure food has become a challenge in the modern world. Foods that are labeled organic can still be mass-produced, possibly using "natural" pesticides which are still toxic. (Purely natural pesticides like bay leaves or marigolds are not harmful, but in my book, biodynamic farming—using living plants to deter bugs—is still the only way to go.) Even worse, companies may claim their food is organic when it's not just to get more money. On the flip side, there is also pure, truly natural food sold without labels and high price tags that is actually organic; it's just that the farmers who grow and sell them can't afford certification as organic farmers.

To be absolutely sure your produce is pure, grow it yourself or forage it in the wild. Planting trees, growing a garden, and especially growing sprouts are all excellent ways to obtain food. Foraged foods are most ideal since nature grew them on its own. Participating in local herb walks and interviewing docents can both provide a solid education about the habitats and seasonal availability of local foods.

Farmers' markets are usually the next best source of fresh produce. They're also a great place to learn about local produce that's available for foraging. In fact, many farmers' markets have a side selection of foods that grow wild in the area; look here for information and inspiration. Farmers also sell directly from their farms so check the phone book for local resources and stop at local farm stands. What the farmers don't sell themselves will go to the shelf of a local store or co-op; ask around and find local markets that buy produce directly from local farms.

For exotic and hard-to-find items, check Asian or Mexican markets as they usually carry a wide range of tropical produce and special items. There are also some companies that mail order exotic foods and fresh produce direct from farms, so no matter where you live, you should be able to find a nice array of produce.

Herbs

Herbs are the greens and flowers of annually blooming plants commonly used for seasoning and medicine. Used both fresh and dried.

Basil—A sweet, broad-leafed aromatic herb that grows rapidly. Some varieties are purple basil, French basil, Thai basil, and lemon basil. Basil is commonly used in Italian and Thai cooking.

Cilantro—A flat-leafed herb widely used in Latin American and Southeast Asian cooking. Sometimes called Mexican parsley, fresh coriander, or Chinese parsley. This plant's seeds are known as coriander.

Dill—A soft, wispy, refreshing herb.

Fennel—A wispy herb similar in appearance to dill, with a slightly sweet licorice taste and smell.

Lamb's-quarter—A common herb found throughout the Northeast and Northwest areas of the United States.

Lemongrass—A long, hearty, sharp-edged green grass with a lemonlike scent.

Lovage—A sweet, beautiful flowering herb with a strong scent.

Malva—A slightly bitter, richly green herb.

Marjoram—A pungent and aromatic herb.

Mint—A refreshing and cool herb that's available in many varieties and grows almost anywhere.

Apple mint—A sweet mint with a slight apple taste and round leaves.

Chocolate mint—A superbly rich mint with tiny, dark leaves.

Lemon mint—A mild mint with a distinct lemon aroma.

Peppermint—A strong, darkly colored mint with smooth, long leaves.

Pineapple mint—A mild, sweet-tasting mint with a hint of pineapple to its taste.

Spearmint—A light-colored, mild, cooling mint with pointed leaves.

Oregano—A mildly sharp-flavored herb available broadleaf or creeping and often used in Italian recipes.

Parsley—A clean-tasting, refreshing herb available curly or flat and high in vitamin C.

Peppergrass—A thin grass with a mildly spicy pepper flavor.

Purslane—A common, round-leafed herb that is quite nice in salads.

Rosemary—A piney, minty herb resembling evergreen needles.

Sage—A robust, pungent, aromatic herb with long, whitish, fuzzy leaves.

Sheep sorrel—An herb with a tangy flavor and high in vitamin C and potassium.

Sourgrass—A wild type of sorrel with yellow flowers, a lemony flavor, and a slight bite.

Tarragon—A tart, mild herb that tastes of anise.

Thyme—An earthy-flavored herb that comes in over forty varieties.

Wintercress—An herb with a slightly spicy, slightly bitter taste, often found growing in moist areas.

Edible Flowers

There are many types of edible flowers found all over the world. They go wonderfully in salads or as a garnish on any dish. Make sure you use only unsprayed, organically raised blossoms in your food. Edible flowers have a very short shelf life so it is best to grow them yourself either in a garden outdoors or in a window box.

Arugula—A delicate, pale lavender or white blossom with a slightly spicy taste.

Borage—A blue, star-shaped flower with a mild, watery, cucumber flavor.

Calendula—A yellow-orange flower that is sweet and calming to the nervous system. It is also known as pot marigold.

Chrysanthemum—A silvery white flower with a slightly spicy taste.

Day lily—A yellow-orange flower. The petals of this plant are edible, while the young buds are not. Day lilies have a nutty, sweet taste.

Garlic—A white or purple flower from the garlic chive with a spicy, garlicky taste.

Geranium—A mild-tasting flower available in many varieties, such as rose, lemon, almond, and mint.

Hibiscus—A bright red, orange, or pink flower that makes wonderful sun tea.

Honeysuckle—A deliciously sweet, honey-flavored, yellow-white tiny flower.

Impatiens—A five-petaled, pastel-colored flower with a mildly sweet taste.

Lavender—A flower with a blue-purple blossom that tastes almost as strong as it smells.

Nasturtium—A very spicy flower available in a variety of colors, from yellow to bright red.

Pansy—A velvety-textured, mild-flavored flower available in many colors.

Red clover—A purple-and-white-topped flower that can be grown from clover seed or found in fields in the early summer. This herb contains high quantities of vitamin C.

Rose—A soft, sweet, aromatic flower.

Scotch broom—A sweet, honey-flavored, bright yellow flower.

Squash—A tender, huge, orange flower with a sweet and slightly starchy taste.

Tiger lily—An exquisite orange flower that tastes like sweet crispy lettuce.

Violet—A purple-pink flower with both sweet and spicy overtones. The flowers, stems, and leaves of the violet are all edible and contain vitamins A and C.

Sea Vegetables

Sea vegetables have an abundance of minerals and trace elements. They are an ideal source of organic salts. They are high in calcium, iodine, potassium, magnesium, phosphorous, iron, niacin, and vitamins A, B^1, B^2, B^6, B^{12}, and C. Sea vegetables are very helpful in cleaning the prostate and the whole lymphatic system. Although eating fresh sea vegetables is ideal, sea vegetables can be purchased dried and then soaked to rehydrate.

Some companies boil their vegetables before drying them. Check the labels carefully; if they don't specify that the vegetables were or were not boiled, find another brand or call the company's customer service number and ask. Always read the package and look for kosher certification to verify that it contains no animal or fish products. Purchase dried sea vegetables at Asian markets or directly from Gold Mine Natural Food Co. (www.goldminenaturalfood.com).

Agar-agar—A clear, gelatinous seaweed product available in flakes or bars. Agar-agar is used to gel liquids into a more solid form.

Arame—A dark brownish green, broad-leafed sea plant most commonly shredded into fine strands. This sweet, nutty sea vegetable is abundant in calcium, phosphorous, iodine, iron, potassium, and vitamins A and B. (Grows around Japan, the Pacific coasts, and South America.)

Dulse—A leafy, purple sea frond from cold northern Atlantic waters that can be eaten dried or rehydrated. Its flat, fan-shaped fronds have a chewy consistency. Dulse has a very high concentration of iron. It is an excellent source of magnesium and potassium and is quite rich in iodine, calcium, phosphorous, vitamins A, B^2, B^6, C, E, and many trace minerals. (Grows in cold waters worldwide.)

Hijiki—A stringy black seaweed that looks like twine. It is thicker and stronger-tasting than arame and is very high in calcium. It also has ample amounts of vitamins A, B^1, B^2, phosphorous, and iron. (Grows in waters around southern Japan, Hawaii, Taiwan, and the Indian Ocean.)

Kombu (kelp)—A green seaweed with chewy, sweetish blades that is dried and used as a condiment or flavor enhancer. Kombu is rich in potassium, sodium, and vitamins A and B. Monosodium glutamate (MSG) is derived from kombu. Dried kelp is available in strips, flakes, and in powdered form as well as vinegared and shredded, giving it a breadlike flavor. (Found in cold waters worldwide, including Japan, northern and mid-Pacific coast, and Atlantic coast.)

Nori—A bright, light purple when growing, this flat-bladed sea vegetable dries purple or black-green. Nori is most commonly found shredded and pressed into sheets and used in sushi. Nori is an excellent source of calcium, potassium, manganese, magnesium, and phosphorous and is especially rich in niacin and protein. Nori also contains large amounts of vitamins A and C. (Grows in the colder waters of the Atlantic and Pacific and along the coasts of Japan, California, Hawaii, the Philippines, and Europe.)

Sea palm—A sea frond that is gray-green with vertical ridges. It is quite firm and slightly jellylike.

Wakame—A dark green seaweed that is sweet and becomes a beautiful light green when rehydrated. It is quite slippery when wet. Wakame is an abundant source of calcium and niacin and is high in vitamins A, B^1, B^2, and C. (Grows in the cold waters of the northern Atlantic and Pacific including the coasts of northern Japan, the United States, and the British Isles.)

Algae

An organism that transforms sunlight into chlorophyll, algae is a substance known for its blood-building and cleansing properties. Algae is abundant in trace minerals, and very digestible and easily assimilated because of its simplicity. Many people use algae supplements for their high amino acid content, naturally available protein, and high levels of trace minerals. The powder and liquid forms of single-celled algae are the only raw options; algae flakes contain soy lecithin, which in its preparation is steamed at temperatures 140°F and higher.

Chlorella—A powdered algae originally discovered by Christopher Hills and Hirashi Nakamura, renowned scientists whose research provided a lot of information about algae to the West.

Phytoplankton—A sea variety of algae that grows in deep waters and still produces chlorophyll from water-filtered sunlight. Phytoplankton is no longer commercially available.

Spirulina—A spiral-shaped algae known for its potency and easy digestibility. Dried spirulina powder is the highest source of protein known, containing almost 70 percent fully absorbable proteins.

Mushrooms

Not all mushrooms are fit for raw consumption. Use caution when harvesting any wild mushroom. Mushrooms can provide a rich and meaty texture that is satisfying to people transitioning to a vegetarian diet.

Chicken-of-the-woods—A thick, yellow-orange, many-layered tree fungus with a fibrous texture. Used fresh.

Enoki (enokidake)—A tiny, slim, white mushroom that often grows in clusters. Used fresh.

Hen-of-the-woods—A light gray tree fungus that grows in bunches similar to chicken-of-the-woods. Used fresh.

Kombucha—A flat fungus grown in a jar or tank of water with green tea and a sweetener. A well-cared-for kombucha colony will continuously divide and multiply, producing an endless supply of kombucha-infused tea if desired. Kombucha tea is known for its healing properties.

Morels—A spongy, wrinkly, brown-black wild mushroom with an elongated head. Used fresh and dried.

Maitake—A small-capped mushroom well known for its immune-building and cancer-fighting abilities. Used fresh and dried.

Portobello—A large, tender mushroom with a smooth, white-brown surface and white stem. Used fresh.

Shiitake—A small, butter-flavored mushroom used in Oriental recipes. Used fresh and dried.

Silver ear—A silver-white fungus that looks like a sponge or coral. Used fresh and dried.

Straw—A very fleshy mushroom. Used fresh (avoid canned).

Tree ear—A dark, round fungus. The smaller varieties are known to be the tastiest. Used fresh.

Truffles—A very rare (and therefore expensive), wild delicacy. A must for the mushroom connoisseur. Used fresh and dried.

Wood ear—A small, gold-brown fungus with a woody flavor. Used fresh.

Legumes

Also known as beans, legumes grow in pods, mostly on vines.

Adzuki beans—A red-skinned dried bean with a sweet flavor when sprouted.

Black beans—A dried black bean with a starchy flavor when sprouted.

Garbanzo beans (chickpeas)—A beige, dimpled dried bean, very good for sprouting.

Kidney beans—A variety of red-skinned legumes that are kidney shaped. These dried beans have a bland taste when sprouted.

Lentil—A traditional ingredient in Indian cuisine, the lentil is a small, flat, and round bean that is sold dried. Lentils come in many colors, are high in protein, and make for very sweet sprouts.

  Green lentils—When sprouted, good in salads.

  Red lentils—Use sprouted in soups and sauces.

  Yellow lentils—Good for making sprout loaves and pâtés.

Lima bean—A large, green-yellow, kidney-shaped bean, with a sweet taste when fresh. Available both fresh and dried.

Mung bean—A fresh, yellow- or green-skinned bean whose sprouts are used frequently in Asian cuisine.

Navy bean—A white dried bean with a mild taste when sprouted.

Pea—A green, round legume with a deliciously sweet flavor when fresh. Dried varieties are also available. Also makes great sprouts.

Peanut—A legume often referred to as a nut, this fresh bean has a rich, nutty flavor.

Pole bean—A fresh, long, pod bean that is crisp and sweet.

Snap pea—A fresh, superbly sweet bean. These crunchy little bright green pods are delicious in salads.

Snow pea—A traditional Chinese pea pod that is sold fresh and is slightly blander than the snap pea.

Soybean—A powerhouse of protein, the soybean is extremely versatile. In either fresh or dried form, the soybean provides the basis for tofu, soymilk, miso, tamari, and many other products.

String bean—A fresh, long, thin, crispy, green pod with small beans inside.

Wax bean—A fresh, long, thin, yellow pod similar to the string bean.

Greens

Leafy green plants grow in heads in a huge array of colors, flavors, and textures. They are rich in chlorophyll, silica, and fiber.

Arugula—A peppery green with a slightly spicy flavor.

Bamboo shoots—The young shoots of certain types of bamboo are edible.

Beet greens—A plant with dark green leaves with a red vein. It tastes mildly bitter, with a woodsy flavor.

Bele (tree spinach)—A plant with large, broad leaves from the Philippines. This plant's tough gelatinous leaves are almost 30 percent silica and are great for rolling burritos.

Chard—A member of the beet family, chard has coarse leaves and a woodsy taste.

Chicory—A dark green plant (often found in the wild) with narrow, frilly leaves, a pale green center, and a bitter flavor.

Comfrey—A plant with broad, fuzzy leaves that can aid in cellular regeneration and the healing of wounds and muscle and bone injuries. Best for raw consumption when the leaves are young and tender.

Dandelion—A bitter green with small and narrow dark leaves. Look for dandelions growing in the wild.

Curly endive—A crisp, light green to white compact head with frilly leaves and a slightly bitter flavor.

Escarole—A broader, less bitter, and curlier green than endive. Escarole is part of the chicory family.

Fiddlehead fern—Often wild, this young sprouted fern has curly light fronds and a delectable nutty, asparagus flavor.

Frisée—A bitter, light yellow to white salad green with curly leaves.

Green butter lettuce—A crispy, large-headed lettuce with generous, wide leaves.

Green leaf lettuce—A loose-headed green with frilly edges and a mild taste.

Green oak lettuce—A loose-headed green with frilly, tapering finger leaves.

Katuk—An African tree whose leaves are more than 30 percent protein and taste like nuts.

Mâche—A mild and delicate green with small, round leaves.

Malabar spinach—A purple and green variety of garden spinach.

Mizuna—A jagged-leafed, slightly spicy green often used in Asian foods.

Mustard—A very pungent, spicy, tart green abundant in vitamins A and B.

New Zealand spinach—A crispy vinelike spinach that grows wild.

Plantain—A long-leaved plant that is common in North America.

Radicchio—A type of red chicory, radicchio has a loose white head and tangy crimson leaves.

Red butter lettuce—A crispy, large-headed lettuce with a red tinge.

Red chard—A large, leafy green with a red vein running up its middle. A member of the beet family.

Red hibiscus—These burgundy-colored leaves have a lemony taste. Red hibiscus can often be found growing in the wild.

Red oak lettuce—A loose-headed green with frilly, red-tinged, tapering, fingerlike leaves.

Red orach—A blossoming, burgundy-colored green with mild flavor.

Savory—A distinctly peppery green with a spicy flavor.

Spinach—A deep green plant whose delicate leaves have a rich, earthy flavor.

Tango—A pungent and flavorful green with a rich flavor.

Tat soi—A round, crispy green with a sweet taste.

Travissio—A sweet and spicy green.

Watercress—A round-leafed, fast-growing green with a bitter aftertaste.

Roots

Roots are starchy, nourishing plants that grow underground. Most root greens are edible and highly nutritious. A root can be cut into a few pieces which, if put in the ground, will each grow new full roots (each piece must include some portion of the roots's external surface).

Beet—A large, bulbous root with red and green leaves.

    Chioga—A red-and-white-ringed beet that looks tie-dyed inside.

    Golden—A golden variety that makes a beautiful decoration.

    Red—A common variety of beet quite high in iron.

Carrot—A long, orange root with a wispy green top.

Celery—A large root with multiple stalks that are high in water and organic sodium content and have small leafy greens on the tips.

Chinese artichoke—A small, white root.

Ginger—A beige root with a sweet and spicy flavor grown in riverbeds.

Ginseng—A gummy root in a variety of colors. Especially value for its energy-boosting and yang-tonifying characteristics.

Jicama—A large, light brown root with a white, crispy inside.

Lotus—A conical tuber that contains hollow tubes in a ring.

Parsnip—A bitter, white root—very nice when shredded.

Potato—A smooth-skinned, eye-covered root that grows prolifically.

    Golden russet—A golden watery potato (very starchy raw).

    Purple—A dark-skinned, purple-fleshed dry potato.

    Red Romano—A red-skinned, white-fleshed, very starchy potato.

Radishes

    Daikon—A long, large, white, crispy, spicy root.

    Horseradish—A very spicy white root.

    Red—A round, red-skinned, juicy radish.

    White—A slightly spicier version of the red.

Rutabaga—A purple-and-white-skinned crispy root with a watery taste.

Salsify—A brown, long, skinny, slightly hairy root.

Sweet potato—An orange-fleshed, very sweet root.

Taro—A dense tuber that causes intense mouth and throat discomfort when eaten raw.

Turmeric—A pungent, bitter, orange root used often in Indian food.

Turnip—A spicy and bitter, large, round, white root.

Yakon—A sweet root related to potatoes, with an apple flavor.

Yam—A very similar root to the sweet potato in taste and appearance.

Yucca—A plant also known as cassava that is too dense and starchy to eat raw.

Brassica

These hardy plants grow in cooler climates in clusters flanked by leaves. They are coated with layers of acidophilus, which helps increase intestinal flora.

Broccoli—A green, clustered, flowerlike plant with some purple overtones that is very high in calcium.

Brussels sprout—A plant that looks like miniature, tight cabbages growing on a stalk.

Cabbage—An acidophilus-rich plant that grows in cooler climates.

Bok choy (Chinese chard)—A cabbage with thick white stalks and broad, dark green leaves.

Choy sum—A cabbage similar to bok choy with a more slender appearance.

Miniature red—A smaller version of the normal red.

Napa (Chinese cabbage)—A plant with layers of dark green, purple-veined leaves.

Red—A cabbage with deep magenta leaves on a compact head.

Savoy—A cabbage with crinkly, pale green leaves and a loose head.

White—A dense, firm head with smooth, yellow-green leaves.

Cauliflower—A white, flowerlike plant with a creamy taste.

Kale—A dark green to purple plant with overlapping leaves and red-purple veins.

Kohlrabi—A round and green plant with a purple stem.

Turnip—A plant with tart leaves and a spicy root.

Allium

Allium are pungent, bulblike plants that grow underground and produce green shoots. They are anthelmintic—they help remove intestinal parasites.

Asparagus—A plant with long branches that end in flowerlike tops with a robust taste.

Chive—A delicate, slender, mild-tasting plant with an onion flavor.

Garlic—A white-skinned bulb composed of cloves individually wrapped in a parchmentlike membrane and with a spicy, often strong flavor.

Leeks—A grasslike plant with a slight onion flavor.

Onions

Kula—An oblong, very sweet onion with a white interior and yellow skin.

Red—A spicy onion with purple-red skin.

Spanish—A yellow-skinned, slightly spicy round onion.

White—A crisp and sweet onion with a white skin.

Scallions—A long, green, grasslike shoot.

Shallots—A small brown bulb with a taste between garlic and onion.

Nightshades

Nightshade plants grow at night and produce a fruit with fine-lobed ears and edible flowers of various colors.

Artichoke—A flowerlike, green plant with sharp leaves.

Eggplant—A large, purple fruit with a light green, seeded interior.

Okra—A pointed, cylindrical green to purple fruit.

Peppers

Hot

Anaheim—A long, mild, thin, fresh green chile.

Cayenne—A long and winding orange to red, pointed, dried chile.

Chile—A small, round-tipped red pepper.

Chipotle—A smoked and dried jalapeño with a smoky flavor and spicy aftertaste.

Habanero—An extremely hot fresh chile whose small size belies its fiery taste.

Jalapeño—A medium-sized fresh green chile with a nice, gentle spice.

Scotch bonnet—An orange, bell-shaped, very hot fresh chile.

Tepín—A medium-hot, red to green dried chile.

Thai—A tiny, red-purple pepper that's super spicy.

Sweet

Green—A crispy, watery, bell pepper.

Orange—A pepper that, aside from its color, is very similar to the red.

Purple—A bland, almost bitter, purple-skinned bell pepper.

Red—A very sweet and crunchy bell pepper.

Yellow—A very sweet and quite juicy bell pepper.

Tomatoes

Beefsteak—A large, watery, light red to pink tomato.

Cherry—A tiny, round, very sweet and juicy tomato.

Pear—A pear-shaped, small tomato that grows in a variety of colors.

Plum—A medium-sized red tomato.

Roma—An oblong and light red tomato, great for slicing.

Curcubits (Vine Squash and Melons)

Circubits are fruits that grow on vines and contain many seeds. All flowers from curcubits are edible.

Acorn squash—A large green and brown squash resembling an acorn.

Melons

Cantaloupe—A commonly known melon, the cantaloupe has fairly dense orange to pink flesh with beige, scaly or bumpy skin.

Crenshaw—A lightly scaly-skinned, golden-fleshed melon that is the ultimate in juiciness.

French—A golden orange–fleshed melon that is a very sweet type of cantaloupe with smooth, beige skin.

Honeydew—A smooth, firm, green-yellow-skinned melon with pale green, ultrasweet flesh.

Honeyloupe—A cross between a cantaloupe and a honeydew, this fine treat has a smooth, firm skin and sweet, pale orange flesh.

Muskmelon—A melon with a scaly, netted skin and extremely sweet, yellow-orange to yellow-green flesh.

Sharlyn—A melon with skin like a cantaloupe, this ultrasweet melon has golden-orange flesh.

Sugar baby—A delectable, smaller, ultrasweet, seedless version of watermelon.

Watermelon—A large melon with a smooth, green or dark yellow, mottled or striped skin and crisp, pink to red flesh composed of 96 percent water. A great kidney cleanser.

Yellow baby—A strain of watermelon that has a creamy yellow flesh.

Pumpkin—A large, rounded, orange squash with many seeds.

Yellow squash—A sweet and crunchy, yellow-skinned summer squash with a mild taste.

Zucchini—A long, green summer squash with an earthy flavor.

Seeds

A seed is defined by the fact that its hull can be removed, and that it produces two leaves upon sprouting. Seeds are the potential energy of plants-to-be and as such have highly increased nutritional value. Seeds can be used in a variety of forms. Store-bought seeds are a dried food and are concentrated. If seeds are soaked, their enzyme inhibitors release and they become more digestible. This can also be accomplished by grinding a seed into powder or by chewing very well. Sprouting seeds is a great way to get more bang for your buck: it increases the seeds' nutritional value as well as their size, thereby providing more food mass.

Alfalfa—A seed that sprouts quickly and provides many valuable nutrients.

Buckwheat—A black-hulled grain that produces sweet greens. Buckwheat is the highest in protein of any seed.

Celery—A seed that helps to inhibit molds and is useful to add to other seeds for sprouting.

Chia—A seed that produces a gelatinous coating before sprouting and is packed with energy.

Clover—A seed that provides a chlorophyll-rich sprout.

Coriander—A seed with a mildly spicy flavor.

Cumin—A robust-tasting seed that is quite earthy.

Fennel—A seed with a distinctive licorice flavor.

Fenugreek—This seed produces a rich and tasty sprout that is great in salads.

Flax—A seed that creates a gelatinous coating when soaked. Provides a good balance of omega oils and essential fatty acids and works well as an egg substitute.

Garlic—A very spicy seed with a reddish hue when sprouted.

Hemp—A rich, tangy seed, high in essential fatty acits

Mustard—A versatile seed that makes great sprouts and is used dry as a spice.

Onion—A sweet and spicy seed, great for sprouting.

Poppy—A round, blue seed with a delightfully crunchy texture.

Pumpkin—A very robust and sweet seed that provides a good balance of omega oils and essential fatty acids.

Radish—A spicy and bitter seed, good for sprouting.

Sesame—A very sweet, tiny, white seed.

Sunflower—A pointed, gray seed, great for making Essene bread and pâtés.

Wild rice—Black long-grain wild rice is the only rice that is a seed and not a grain. This seed also sprouts without any oxygen.

Grains

Grains are the kernel of a plant that produces only one shoot, a grass. Grains are permanently affixed to their hull and usually contain gluten. These close relatives of seeds are abundant in carbohydrates and most digestible when sprouted.

Amaranth—A grain native to the Americas and the second-smallest grain, amaranth plants grow soft red and white flowers. The seeds sprout easily.

Corn—A starchy, sweet, juicy grain that grows in a number of colors. Wonderful both raw and sprouted.

Millet—A small, yellow grain with a starchy taste when sprouted.

Oat—A very sweet grain to sprout. Lots of fiber.

Quinoa—A grain worshipped by the Aztecs, quinoa is the third-smallest grain and creates a spicy sprout.

Rice—The staple grain of China. Most rices are edible when sprouted, though not very tasty. Experiment with the length of sprout time for varied flavors.

Basmati—A translucent long grain.

Brown long grain—A long, round, brown grain.

Brown short grain—A short, stubby, brown grain.

Jasmine—A white, sweet rice with a delicate fragrance.

Spanish—A long, yellow rice.

Sushi—A white, round grain used in the making of sushi.

Sweet—A white, stubby grain.

Rye—A brown seed good for making Essene bread.

Teff—A very small grain, sweet and gray. High in protein.

Wheat—A grass rich in chlorophyll. The staple grain of America, it produces a tasty sprout.

Hard winter—A good variety for growing wheatgrass.

Soft winter—A wheat that is very good for making Essene bread.

Summer—A sweeter wheat variety. Good for making breads and salads.

Nuts

Nuts are the inner center of a fruit that is contained by a shell. Nuts are very sweet when harvested and get much more oily when dried.

Almond—A white, oblong nut, pointed on one end, that comes in a beige shell.

Brazil—A creamy, oily nut that is often an inch in length.

Cashew—A white, very sweet, crescent-shaped nut that is poisonous unless sun dried.

Chestnut—A brown-skinned, large, round, crunchy nut that is sometimes bitter.

Hazelnut—A dark brown–skinned, small, round nut with a rich flavor.

Macadamia—A sweet, white nut with a delightful crunch and a very hard shell.

Malabar chestnut—A light brown–skinned, sweet nut that is crispy when sprouted.

Pecan—An oblong-shelled nut with a wavy interior. This nut is very sweet.

Pine—A golden, tiny, teardrop-shaped seed from a pine cone. It tastes quite rich.

Walnut—A round-shelled and warped-shaped nut.

Fruits

Fruit is a beautiful, colorful, delicious membrane made of cells filled with organic water and nutrients. Fruit is love since it is designed to feed the seed inside or feed a creature and with that creature's cooperation spread the seeds around the local area making more fruit trees and more fruit. Fruits come in every flavor and color.

Annona or moya family—Annonaceous fruits have scaly skins, black seeds, and creamy flesh.

Atemoya—A hybrid between the sweetsop and cherimoya.

Bullock's heart—A purple-skinned fruit consisting of an exterior with rounded scales and an interior flesh that is sweet and creamy.

Cherimoya—A sweet and juicy version of the sweetsop, with far fewer seeds.

Rollinia deliciosa—A black and gold, spiky fruit with the sweet flavor of lemon pudding.

Soursop—A spiky, green fruit also known as the guanabana, with a sour and sweet white flesh and many poisonous seeds that must be removed before consumption.

Sweetsop—A green, round, scaly fruit also known as the sugar apple, with a seed-filled interior and a sweet and creamy taste.

Apples

Discovery—A red apple that fruits late in the season.

Gala—A medium-sized, crisp, juicy apple, with skin that is mostly red with some yellow.

Golden Delicious—A golden, sun-filled apple with a sweet taste.

Granny Smith—A green, hard apple with a sweet-tart taste.

Jonagold—A golden apple with a mild flavor.

McIntosh—A small, red and white apple that is good when soft.

Pippin—A crispy and crunchy apple with red skin.

Red Delicious—A large, red apple with a sweet flavor and a hard crunch.

Spartan—A medium-sized, red and green apple with a mildly sour taste.

Starkling Delicious—A small, red and gold apple.

Asian pear—A beige-skinned, sweet fruit that has a taste and texture similar to a pear but looks like an apple.

Avocados

Alligator pear—A watery, light-colored, small, slender avocado.

Bacon—A rich bacon-flavored avocado with dark green, smooth skin.

Cocktail avocado—A sweet avocado that is the smallest of its kind.

Common—A round, hard-skinned avocado with creamy insides.

Ettinger—A green, mildly rough-skinned avocado with creamy flesh.

Fuerte—A watery avocado with a sometimes purple, smooth skin.

Hass—A dark, rough-skinned avocado with a buttery taste. One of the most popular varieties.

Napal—A large and purple avocado whose flavor varies from tree to tree.

Reed—A round, green-skinned, sweet and creamy avocado.

Sharwil—A green-skinned, dry, buttery avocado.

Bananas

Apple—A small, starchy banana with a reddish interior.

Bluefield—This is the largest, fattest, and sweetest of its kind.

Chinese—A long and very sweet banana. Slightly thinner than the Bluefield variety.

Cuban red—A red, semistarchy, semisweet banana.

Dessert—A medium-sized, sweet and creamy banana.

Ice cream—A large, triangular banana with white flesh reminiscent of vanilla ice cream.

Lady finger—A tiny and supersweet banana.

Plantain—A dry and starchy banana.

Berries

Black raspberry—A medium-sized berry formed of many black beads.

Blackberry—A black, seed-filled berry with a very strong, slightly sour taste.

Blueberry—A small, blue bush berry with a sweet taste. A very high source of pectin.

Boysenberry—A sweet, purple berry.

Cranberry—A very tangy and sour red berry.

Currant

  Black—A very sweet berry often eaten dried.

  Red—A slightly more tart, red variety.

  White—A whitish yellow variety.

Dewberry—A sweet, tiny cousin of the raspberry.

Gooseberry—A green bush berry related to the blueberry.

Mulberry—A black, sweet berry that has a sweet and sour flavor and grows on trees.

Physalis fruits

  Chinese lantern—A tiny, yellow, sweet, tomato-like fruit coated with a papery skin.

  Tomatillo—A green-purple, very sweet, tomato-like fruit also covered with a papery husk.

Raspberry—A red, very sweet, oblong fruit from a bush that grows in cold climates.

Strawberry—A red, pointed berry that has a distinct taste and grows on low ground shrubs.

  Alpine—A white variety not as sweet as the traditional raspberry.

  Hot boy—A very crimson berry with a tart bite.

  Red gauntlet—A large, red variety with a high sugar content.

  Scarlet—A dark red, very sweet, medium-sized berry.

  White—A white to yellow, tiny berry.

  Wild—A miniature berry with little flavor that grows in small clusters in the shade.

Tayberry—A very sweet and mild berry also known as the thimbleberry.

Breadfruit—A round, scaly fruit that tastes like a bread pudding when eaten very ripe.

Cacao—Food of the gods. Cacao pods, ranging in color from yellow to purple and resembling a papaya in shape, contain both a sweet, white pulp and a number of small seeds. The seeds, when dried and roasted, are the source of chocolate.

Carob—Carob pods are nature's candy bar: they taste like chocolate-covered caramel. The seeds are as hard as rocks, so remove them before eating or navigate around them carefully.

Cherries

Barbados—A black, small cherry with a large seed.

Bing—A very tangy cherry.

Dukes—A large, black cherry with a rich taste.

Early rivers—A red cherry that is quite sweet.

Surinam—A small, light red, sour cherry shaped like a small pumpkin.

Citrus, sour

Calmondin—A tiny, very sour orange.

Citron—A medium-sized, yellow fruit with lemony flavor.

Kumquat—A small, orange fruit with a sweet and sour flavor.

Lemon—A sour fruit with golden juice and skin.

Ugli fruit—A rough-skinned version of the lemon.

Meyer lemon—A sweeter and juicier lemon.

Limes

Green—A green-skinned fruit with sour flavor and sweet undertones.

Kaffir—A small pear-shaped lime, whose leaves, which are uniquely shaped like two leaves joined end to end, are often used in Asian cuisines.

Tiny—A round, yellow to green, small lime.

Yellow—A yellow-orange variety.

Orangequat—A sour orange with mild flavor.

Citrus, sweet

Grapefruit

Pink grapefruit—A slightly more sour version of the red.

Pomelo—A very large and thick-skinned grapefruit.

Ruby red—A red-fleshed, very sweet variety of grapefruit.

Oranges

Blood—A red-and-orange-skinned, very sweet fruit.

Clementine—A tangy and juicy orange.

Mandarin—A tiny and tart orange.

Mineola—A very juicy, sweet orange.

Navel—A very round and mild orange.

Satsuma—A small, Oriental variety with a tangy aftertaste.

Seville—A sweet, golden-fleshed variety.

Sour—A sour version of the navel orange.

Valencia—A very common variety that is easy to cultivate.

Tangelo—A cross between a tangerine and an orange.

Tangerine—A very dark orange in color, with soft, sweet fruit. Resembles a squished orange.

Unique fruit—A rough-skinned, sour fruit.

Coconut—A hard-shelled fruit of a palm tree that contains both water that is high in electrolytes and a white gelatinous meat that is very rich and protein packed.

Coconuts are the fruit of a palm that has been around since prehistoric times. This prolific plant has made it to the shore of every continent except Antarctia and is available in over 100 varieties. Coconuts can float for three months in the ocean and land on a sandy beach and still sprout up a tree that will bear up to ten thousand coconuts in its lifetime.

Coconuts can be used at almost any stage of ripeness. Baby or bitter coconuts are used for their water as they have not yet developed any meat. The water in these young nuts is slightly bitter and is considered medicinal in many island nations around the world as well as throughout Asia. As they develop slightly sweeter water and a small amount of clear jelly on the inside of their shell, baby coconuts are then called jelly nuts or spooners. Next, the coconut graduates to young or green coconuts, the most popular variety for use in food and for drinking. These young nuts have very sweet water and a coating of rich, creamy, soft meat a centimeter or more thick on their inside shell.

Mature coconuts are the kind most people are used to seeing in a supermarket. These brown nuts have had most of the husk removed down to the shell layer. These nuts are old and the water is either bad or has fermented and tastes like coconut champagne. Mature coconuts are used for oil and cream made from the hard meat. If a mature nut falls to the ground and has a chance to germinate it becomes a coconut sprout—once considered the most powerful food in the Hawaiian Islands. Sprouted coconuts contain a spongelike heart that tastes like cotton candy. Its meat, known as copra, is very thin and crispy and has a thin layer of natural coconut oil. The oil can be obtained (for nutritional, medicinal, or cosmetic purposes) just by rubbing a finger on the inside of the copra. Coconuts are essential to the raw food diet so it is important to know how to find them at the desired ripeness and then, of course, how to open them. Since there are so many varieties of coconuts, it can be challenging to tell what stage of ripeness a coconut is at. Look for the the three nubs at the base of the nut; if they're close together, the coconut is most likely young (as the nut ages, the nubs spread farther apart). High moisture content in the coconut's husk can also help determine how young a nut is; the higher the moisture content, the younger the coconut since the husk dries out as it ages. Though most young nuts have a green stage, don't be thrown off by color: some nuts are always red, brown, gold, or green.

To open a coconut, using a machete or a heavy knife, shave one side of the coconut's outer layer at a 45° angle, until a hole providing access to the coconut water is created. Reserve or drink the water, then chop the coconut in half lengthwise with the grain. Some industrious people also open coconuts with power drills. At Chinese and Mexican markets, you may find young coconuts sold with their husks removed; typically these nuts don't keep as long or taste as fresh but they are much easier to open. The meat of mature nuts can be scooped out by using the back edge of a butter knife, carefully avoiding the hard shell which isn't fun to eat. To remove the meat from a young coconut, all that's needed is a spoon since the meat is thinner and softer.

Coffee—A small red bean of a tropical tree.

Date—The fruit of a palm that, when fruiting, produces up to three hundred pounds at a time. Dates are used as the primary sweetener in a raw-food diet. Dates range in color from green to golden brown to black depending on ripeness and variety. My favorite varieties are Bahari for its wonderful flavor and Medjool for its large size and nice texture. No matter the variety, choose soft dates, as they're more likely to be fresh and have a better flavor.

Bahari—A very sweet, soft, almost honeylike date.

Bread—A very dry, chewy date.

Deglet Noor—A large and creamy variety.

Halawi—A brown, soft, sweet date.

Honey—A sticky, honey, flavored, golden date.

Medjool—A very sweet date that is one of the largest.

Zahidi—A small, dark date with a taste that has hints of maple.

Durian—A yellow fruit that smells like sulfur but tastes like vanilla ice cream.

Fig—A very sweet, small, plump, pear-shaped fruit filled with many seeds and small fibers. This fruit is delicious fresh and also can be dried. Dried figs are even sweeter and often the fig sugars will crystallize on the outside.

Guavas

Common guava—A hard, yellow-skinned fruit with pinkish flesh and many seeds.

Pineapple guava—A guava also known as the feijoa, that tastes like pineapple.

Quince—A pear-shaped fruit also known as the guava pear.

Strawberry guava—A tiny, red guava filled with a tart, white membrane.

Jaboticaba—A small, black-skinned fruit that is very sweet and grows directly from the trunk of the tree.

Jackfruit—A large, spiky fruit weighing up to seventy pounds that has an edible membrane surrounding a seed that tastes like Juicy Fruit gum.

Kiwi—A small, brown, hairy fruit with distinctive bright green and black insides and a taste that is a cross between strawberry and banana. Peel before eating.

Longan—A fruit also known as the dragon's eye, with a hard, brown skin and a white membrane–covered seed that is quite juicy.

Lychee—A red, rough-skinned fruit similar to the longan although sweeter.

Mabolo—A fruit known as the velvet apple, with a velvety skin and a flavor like apples and bananas.

Mango—A sweet and juicy fruit that is grown in hundreds of varieties around the world and ranges greatly in shape, color, and flavor.

> *Alphonso*—A juicy, orange mango with a honeylike taste.
>
> *Haden*—A sticky, sweet, very orange mango with multicolored flesh.
>
> *Julie*—A small, sweet mango with mild flavor.
>
> *Kent*—A cold-climate mango with a creamy flavor.

Mangosteen—A fruit known as the queen of the fruits, that has a purple skin and a number of white, gelatinous, moon-shaped pods inside.

Miracle fruit—A red and tiny fruit that, when eaten before sour foods, makes them taste sweet for about thirty minutes.

Monstera—The large, tubular fruit of the *Monstera deliciosa* plant, with many green scales. It can only be eaten a little at a time to avoid stinging from the acids in the fruit. It tastes like pineapple and banana.

Papaya—A pear-shaped fruit that contains many black seeds and takes nine months to ripen.

> *Babaco*—A giant, mountain papaya that is mild in flavor.
>
> *Common*—A yellow-skinned and yellow-fleshed, very sweet papaya.
>
> *Strawberry papaya*—A red-fleshed version that is much sweeter than other varieties.

Passion fruit

> *Common*—A yellow-shell fruit filled with a sweet-sour, yellow membrane surrounding many edible seeds.
>
> *Purple*—A purple-shelled variety with a slightly more acidic taste.
>
> *Velvet*—A very sweet, orange, soft-skinned passion fruit with white membranes.

Peanut butter fruit—A small, red fruit also known as a ciruela, that tastes similar to peanut butter.

Pears

  Anjou—A large green pear.

  Bartlett—A red-skinned, very sweet pear.

  Bosc—A beige-skinned pear best eaten soft.

Persimmon—A sweet orange fruit commonly grown in Asia and California.

  Fuyu—A round variety that is like an apple when eaten hard and like a Hachiya (below) when soft.

  Hachiya—A pointed variety that is only eaten when soft. Hachiya are very gelatinous and sweet.

Pineapple—The very juicy and sweet fruit of a small ground bush with sharp leaves. It is known as the "King of the Fruits" because of its crown.

  Common—A variety that grows rapidly and produces medium-sized fruits.

  Sugarloaf—A sweet variety with a beautiful golden color.

  White—A white-fleshed pineapple that has a lower acid content than most pineapples and tastes very creamy.

Prickly pear—A fruit from a variety of cactus, it has a very sweet and melonlike flavor and is filled with seeds. This fruit comes in purple and green and contains very simple sugars that can provide quick energy. If foraging this fruit, beware of its many miniscule barbed thorns. Clean very well before use.

Rambutan—A cousin of the lychee, oblong with red, hairy tendrils all over its exterior.

Sapote—A subtropical, round fruit with a sweet flesh and several seeds that should be removed before using. The eggfruit and sapodilla are both members of the sapote family, but the vanilla sapote (below) is not.

  Chocolate pudding fruit—A fruit with a creamy brown inside and a green skin that tastes like very ripe bananas. It is also known as the chocolate persimmon or black sapote.

  Eggfruit—A rich, orange fruit also called a canistel or yellow sapote, that has very cakelike meat.

  Mamey—A caramel-flavored fruit with brown skin.

  Orange sapote—An orange-fleshed, creamy, oblong fruit.

  Sapodilla—A small, brown-skinned fruit, also called a chico, that tastes like cinnamon and sugar.

  Vanilla sapote—A green-skinned fruit with a white, vanilla pudding–like interior.

Tamarillo—An oblong, red fruit that is also known as the tree tomato and tastes of basil and tomatoes.

Tamarind—A rich seed with a sweet-tart flavor.

Vine fruit

Black Grapes

Flame—A dark purple, sweet grape.

White Grapes

California seedless—A seedless variety of the white grape.

Italia—A strain from Italy often used for wines.

Muscat—A light green grape with a very sweet taste and small seed.

Sultanas—A variety of grape used often in desserts.

Thompson seedless—A darker, seedless variety.

Raw Condiments

These foods are designed to season and flavor your dishes and recipes. Variety is the spice of life so use these to enliven and enhance other foods. These foods are available at local health food stores.

Beet powder—Red beets that have been dehydrated and powdered. Excellent for coloring food.

Bragg Liquid Aminos—An aged soy product used to replace salt.

Carob powder—A soft inner lining of the carob pod.

Cayenne pepper—Dried hot pepper available in a range of Btu's (British thermal units). The lower Btu's are for food and the higher ones are for medicinal usage.

Curry powder—A mixture of Indian spices: curry leaf, coriander, and tumeric.

Dried shredded coconut—Dehydrated coconut meat finely shredded.

Enzyme sprinkle—Dehydrated green papayas and lime juice.

Kelp powder—A dried and powdered form of kombu used as a salty seasoning.

Mirin—A sweet Asian rice wine.

Miso—An aged and cultured soy paste.

Nama shoyu—A fermented soy and wheat sauce.

Nigari—A dried form of sea water that coagulates tofu.

Nutritional yeast—A type of yeast grown on beet sugar that contains a wide range of B vitamins especially B^{12} which is considered challenging for vegetarians to find naturally.

Oil—Any dry nut or seed, olive, or oily fruit (such as coconuts) can be pressed for oil. Be certain to look for cold-pressed oils rather than oils that have been extracted using solvents. Also, be aware that "cold-pressed" is commonly used to describe oils that result from heating ground ingredients to 160°F before pressing. Omega Flow oils are truly cold pressed; ask at your local health food store for other brands if Omega Flow oils aren't available. Oils don't last very long separated from their whole food; store them in a dark container (light may cause spoilage) in the refrigerator. Stable oils (like olive oil) maintain their integrity when heated; unstable oils (like flax oil) become toxic when heated. The oils listed here can be found in the refrigerated or vitamin section of local health food stores.

Avocado oil—It is quite rare to find a cold-extracted avocado oil. However, avocados are often very oily on their own and can be used as a whole food replacement for other oils.

Coconut oil—Coconut oil is one of the best fats you can consume. It is delicious and creamy and can be used both in recipes and as a moisturizer.

Flax oil—Flax oil is high in essential fatty acids and is one of the healthiest oils to eat. Flax has a rich taste and is a delight in sweet and savory dishes.

Hemp seed oil—Hemp seed oil has a very nutty flavor and can be used in place of flax oil. This oil is unstable and should never be heated or used in recipes that are dehydrated.

Nut and seed oils—Dried seeds and nuts can be pressed for their oils. Many commercial nut and seed oils are heated during processing and are therefore not raw. Look for cold-pressed nut and seed oils in specialty stores.

Olive oil—Olive oil is the most stable oil; it can handle slight amounts of heat and is very tasty in recipes.

Other oils—There are a wide variety of oils sold in health food stores that may be far less than healthful. Fractionated or overheated oils become rancid quickly and some oils are even toxic for human consumption.

Stevia—A green herb that is one hundred times sweeter than sugar and is useful as a nonfruit sweetener.

Sun-dried sea salt—This salt looks gray and feels wet. That is because it is slow-dried sea water. Sun-dried sea salt contains far more minerals than table salt.

Vinegar—Always buy vinegar that says "with the mother" on the label because that is a sure sign that it is live and raw.

Apple cider vinegar—A fermented apple product with a tangy taste.

Red wine vinegar—A fermented grape vinegar.

Wasabi—A spicy, condiment made from horseradish roots and gardenia flowers. This bright green paste is served with Japanese food. Wasabi is also available in powdered form.

Raw Tools

The right tool for the right job makes everything easier. Working with the proper culinary tools can add to the beauty of food and allow us to create meals in minutes.

Blender—A tool used to mix, whip, cream, and crush.

Blender cup—A small jar that fits upside down on the blender allowing smaller quantities to be blended at a time. Blender cups also allow for more torque per square inch, thereby providing creamier, smoother blends. Most blender bases (the blade and bottom) have a standard type of threading that will actually attach to any small-mouthed jar, such as an old nut butter or honey jar. (Some hardware stores even carry the right-sized jars new.) The jars can be filled up three-quarters full and once blending is complete, the original lid can be screwed back on for storage.

Ceramic drying tray—A flat, porcelain or ceramic dish used for solar drying.

Cutting board—A wooden cutting board is best. It is nontoxic and food-safe. It does absorb flavors, so it is best to wash between uses or to have separate boards for fruits and vegetables.

Dehydrator—A dehydrator is a machine that allows food to dry at an even rate. Many types of dehydrators are available. The best are those with a fan and a heating element in the rear. Stackable dryers are less efficient and can under- or overdry foods. Excalibur makes a good, home-model, food dryer that is efficient and reliable. Many people even build their own dryers, and in some places people sun dry their food.

Drying screen—A piece of framed mesh rigged so that it can be suspended, maximizing airflow.

Food processor—A wonderful aid in the kitchen. It can chop, dice, and slice large amounts of food very quickly. It is powerful enough to grind nuts and seeds into powder.

Garnishing tool—A variety of tools (anything from small, pointed skewers to V-shaped, sharp, pointed spoons) are available to create garnishes. Look in your local cookware store for inspiration.

Ginger grater—A porcelain tray with a deep rim and many small, sharp nubs used to make ginger juice.

Grater—A tool to shred.

Juicers—Juicers separate organic liquids from foods. Fruits, vegetables, soaked nuts, and sprouts can all be juiced. Juicing concentrates the food's nutrients while removing its fibers, thus providing us with more energy that's more readily absorbed by our bodies (meaning more energy from less food). Be sure to juice only organic or unsprayed foods since otherwise the juicing process will concentrate any pesticides or other chemicals along with the food's nutrients.

Centrifugal—Centrifugal or spinning juicers are juicers that have a spinning metal blade in their upper chamber that shreds and spins off juice. These are the most common juicer available on the market. They are often cheap, easy to clean, and compact. These juicers lack in efficiency though; they give only 60 percent of the juice. (To improve this rate, try running the pulp through a second pass.) Centrifugal juicers also cause the juice to quickly oxidize and the juice may require straining.

Homogenizing—Juicers use the process of mastication to grind and press juice from its source (much like our own teeth). The Champion Juicer (my favorite) is one masticating juicer available today; it grinds its little teeth on a hub and presses the fruits, vegetables, nuts, or seeds up against a screen or blank plate. Any homogenizing juicer can masticate (homogenize) foods into paste or a pulp as well as juice them. Masticating juicers are 80 percent efficient and produce juice that is much slower to oxidize.

Juice press—Juice presses are one of the most efficient ways to extract juice. The juice produced is barely oxidized, tastes the best, and has the longest shelf life and stability.

Automatic—The Norwalk juicer is an electric press, much like the hand press. This machine also comes with a built-in grinder attached to the side for mashing harder vegetables or grinding sprouted grains.

Citrus juicer—Used to press juice out of citrus fruits.

Hand press—These presses are made from two-ton hydraulic car jacks and stainless steel screws, plates, and bowls. The juicy pulp of fruits or veggies is placed in a cloth bag inside a bowl and the juice is then pressed out by pumping a jack. Harder vegetables must be ground before hand juicing.

Juice bag—This simple juicer is inexpensive and lightweight (perfect for travel). Shred hard vegetables or fruits (juicy fruits can just be cut and inserted whole), then place in a mesh sprout bag or cloth. Squeeze over a bowl to catch the juice. This juice has the slowest oxidation rate, but unfortunately the method isn't very efficient.

Screw press—Available manual or electric, these have a spiral screw that presses against a screen, forcing foods through the top, separating the pulp and juice. A wheatgrass juicer is one type of screw press.

Triturating—A triturating juicer is one that uses two gears to grind and press foods for homogenizing. This process is very similar to mastication yet happens at a slower speed. Trituration provides juice that oxidizes very slowly and is 90 percent or more efficient.

Knives

Chef's—A long, wide knife for slicing.

Chopping—A large, heavy knife for mincing and dicing.

Paring—A small knife for peeling and exact cutting.

Mandoline—A device to slice vegetables and fruits in a number of ways—from strips to crinkle cut.

Nori roller—A bamboo mat used to roll up sushi.

Pastry bag—A bag with assorted tips that is filled and used to decorate food.

Spiralizer—A plastic device used to turn firm vegetables into angel hair strands. A great way to make raw pasta.

Sprout bag—A breathable cloth bag used for growing sprouts.

Sprout jar—A jar to grow sprouts, covered with a screen or mesh.

Vitamixer—A powerful blender made of stainless steel with blades that reverse direction.

Water purifier—A means of removing impurities, chemicals, pollutants, and bacteria from water.

Whirister—A small food processor, great for herbs and garnishes.

Zester—A small tool used to grate the skin of citrus.

Raw Techniques

The basic skills discussed in this chapter are the foundation of raw-food preparation. A general understanding of these principals will allow you to create divine delights. These techniques take some time to master.

Soaking Dates, Dried Fruits, and Nuts

Dried foods can be rehydrated to make them easier to use in recipes. To use dates as a sweetener, they often require soaking for an hour or so, then blending until smooth. It is important to remove the seeds from dates before use.

Nuts and seeds from many fruits can be soaked to make them blend up more smoothly. Seeds and nuts contain enzyme inhibitors that limit their digestibility. When we soak seeds and nuts for 15 minutes we release up to 50 percent of the enzyme inhibitors. By soaking the correct amount of time (see sprout chart, page 44) we can release all of the enzyme inhibitors, making the seeds and nuts easier to assimilate. Sprouting a seed or nut will give it more of a watery and sweet taste, so sometimes soaking a nut can be more ideal in a recipe than fully sprouting it. Do not use soaking water from seeds since it contains all of the enzyme inhibitors we are removing. (Soaking water from fruits such as dates or sun-dried tomatoes however, is excellent to use.)

Growing Wheatgrass

Wheatgrass is fun and easy to grow. To sprout wheat, just follow the same directions for sprouting seeds (see page 45), and then spread a thick layer of wheat sprouts on the surface of a tray filled with soil 1½ inches deep or spread the sprouts on the ground. Then, cover the sprouts with a thin layer of soil. Next, cover the tray with mesh or another tray. Water the wheatgrass every day to keep it moist and after 3 days it will push up the top tray. Remove the tray and continue to water as needed. When the grass is about 5 inches tall, expose it to some sunlight for a few hours each day to help enrich the chlorophyll. Wheatgrass is one of the best sources of chlorophyll, containing as much as 70 percent chlorophyll.

There are many varieties of wheat and all have different purposes. Winter wheat is better for wheatgrass, soft spring wheat is best for fermenting, and summer wheat is nice for dehydration and cereal. Many strains of wheat have been used as a staple grain since ancient times.

Fermentation

Fermentation is the process of culturing beneficial bacteria in food. Bacteria, such as acidophilus and those found in foods like koji and miso, are all very helpful in the body's assimilation of food. Friendly bacteria live in the digestive tract and break down food so that it can feed our bodies. There are also harmful cultures that can get inside the body and the best way to get rid of them is to have an abundance of good bacteria. Foods such as sprouted beans, nuts, and seeds all ferment very well when introduced to bacteria and kept in a warm place. Many cultured products can be easily made, such as kim chee, seed cheeze, rejuvelac, and tofu.

Fermented foods are living foods. A living food is one with live bacteria flourishing in it and that contains organisms that can live in the body of an animal in a symbiotic relationship. It is possible to cook a food and then culture it, but raw-foodists believe in sprouting foods to ferment them. It is good to check with local stores as to how the foods were shipped and stored, because cultured foods aren't viable once frozen or heated. Some foods culture in hours and others in days. Some foods can be cultured for years (such as miso and shoyu).

SEED SOAKING AND SPROUTING TIMES

Type of Seed	Amount	Soak Time	Sprout Time* (comments)
Adzuki	1 1/2 cups	8 hours	3 days
Alfalfa	3 tablespoons	6 hours	3 days
Almond	3 cups	8 hours	1 to 2 days
Barley	2 1/2 cups	7 hours	2 to 3 days (plant in soil for grass)
Buckwheat in hull	2 cups	6 hours	2 days (plant in soil for greens)
Buckwheat no hull	2 cups	10 hours	1 day
Cabbage	3 tablespoons	6 hours	3 days
Cashew	3 cups	5 hours	1 day
Chia	3 tablespoons	5 hours	2 to 3 days
Corn	2 cups	8 to 10 hours	3 days
Cumin	1 cup	7 to 9 hours	1 day
Dill	3 tablespoons	5 hours	2 days
Fenugreek	1/2 cup	7 hours	3 days
Flax	3 cups	6 hours	2 to 3 days (1 hour is okay)
Garbanzo	1 1/2 cups	8 hours	2 to 3 days
Hazelnut	2 cups	8 hours	2 to 3 days
Kamut	2 cups	7 hours	2 to 3 days (plant in soil for grass)
Lentil	2 cups	7 hours	3 days
Macadamia	3 cups	5 to 7 hours	4 days
Millet	2 cups	8 hours	3 days
Mung bean	2 cups	8 hours	3 days
Mustard	3 tablespoons	6 hours	2 days
Oat groats	2 1/2 cups	6 hours	2 days
Peanut	2 cups	8 hours	2 days
Peas	2 cups	7 hours	3 days
Pecan	2 1/2 cups	4 hours	–
Quinoa	2 cups	6 hours	1 day
Radish	3 tablespoons	6 hours	3 days
Red clover	3 tablespoons	6 hours	3 days
Rye	2 cups	8 hours	3 days (plant in soil for grass)
Sesame	2 cups	6 hours	2 days
Soy	2 cups	8 hours	3 days (1 day for tofu)
Sunflower	3 cups	7 hours	2 days (plant in soil for grass)
Triticale	2 cups	6 hours	3 days
Walnut	2 1/2 cups	4 hours	–
Wheat	2 cups	7 hours	2 to 3 days (plant in soil for grass)
Wild rice	3 cups	9 hours	3 to 5 days

* *Sprout time is from drain time to time of consumption. The length of sprouting time may vary based on climate. These instructions are for a 1/2-gallon jar or bag.*

Sprouting

Sprouting is the easiest way to grow foods for yourself. All seeds are sproutable. The sprout is the young growth of a seed or nut when the enzyme inhibitors have been released and the food has become enzyme rich. Sprouts are abundantly rich in chlorophyll, quite diverse, and a very high source of protein and other nutrients.

To sprout, first select the type of seed you wish to grow and refer to the chart on page 44 to find out the optimal soaking time. You can sprout seeds in just about any container, though a large glass jar (½ to 1 gallon) with a screen cover is the most popular setup. As a general rule, for a yield of ½ gallon of sprouted seeds, use 2 to 3 tablespoons of small seeds such as alfalfa or clover; 1½ cups of medium seeds such as wheat, oat, and garbanzo; and 2 to 3 cups of nuts and rice. Soak the seeds using the time on the sprouting chart. Next, drain the sprouts. After that, rinse the sprouts with fresh water at least twice a day until the tails are at least three times the size of the seed in length. Next, expose your sprouts, still in the jar, to sunlight for about 15 minutes to activate the abundance of chlorophyll. Now, chow down!

Dehydration

Dehydration is the process of removing the water from food to create densely textured live foods. Each food has a different water content, and therefore drying time varies from food to food. In ancient times food was put in the sun to dry. Today we have more advanced technology at our disposal. The purpose of dehydration is to concentrate the food while leaving the enzymes alive. Enzymes die around 113°F, so to be safe, we dehydrate at around 108°F. For drying breads, I advocate the use of a dehydrator that has both a fan and a temperature control (such as the Excalibur). If a dehydrator is unavailable, an oven set on the lowest temperature with the door slightly ajar will work. You can also place the bread on a screen and suspend it in the air or press the bread on a ceramic tray and leave it in the full sun. Flipping the bread over frequently can help it dry faster. Please help carry on this sacred tradition.
If you are dehydrating outdoors in the sun, the temperature is always fine although warmer temperatures will make dehydration occur more quickly. When making sun-baked foods it is nice to create a screened area to do it in so that no bugs or animals get to the food. (See chart on page 46.)

DEHYDRATION TIMES

Type of Food	Length of Dehydration (comments)
Apple	13 hours
Banana	18 hours
Buckwheat	10 hours
Carrot pulp	8 hours
Coconut	20 hours
Corn	18 hours
Essence breads	12 to 48 hours (rate depends on method)
Flowers	3 to 5 hours (dry at 98°F to keep color)
Flax	12 hours
Garlic	5 hours
Garbanzo bean sprouts	10 hours
Herbs	5 to 7 hours
Kiwi	16 hours
Mango	21 hours
Oat groats	15 to 18 hours (rate depends on method)
Onion	13 hours
Papaya	16 hours
Pear	15 hours
Peach	18 hours
Persimmon	18 hours
Pineapple	21 hours
Potatoes	16 hours
Sapodilla	12 hours
Sea vegetables	15 hours
Sprouts (most varieties)	13 hours
Star fruit	13 hours
Tomato	18 hours

Garnishing

Garnishing is the art of beautifying foods. There are so many possible colors and shapes to work with. Use your creativity. There are many different tools. A peeler can be used to peel the skin of a tomato to produce a thin strip that can be rolled up to look like a rose. A sharp spoon can be used to carve root vegetables into many shapes and sculptures. There are also standard tools, such as the radish roser, that produces a rose out of a radish, or a tomato scooper that perfectly takes out the seeds of a tomato. The Japanese have discovered some of the most beautiful ways to garnish foods and there are a variety of books on the subject. By garnishing a food, the presentation is enhanced and that adds to the enjoyment of the food. Remember, eating is an experience and each part of it, from atmosphere to taste, color, and garnishing all play a large part in the pleasure it provides.

Composting and Recycling

In today's world it is ideal to walk as lightly as possible upon the Earth. We have learned that the Earth's resources are exhaustible and that pollution is damaging. By attempting to produce less waste we help make the future brighter. Almost everything is recyclable; whether it is used again or broken down and made into something new, it is still one less tree chopped or chemical created. Composting is beautiful, as it both eliminates all organic waste in a conscious way and refertilizes the soil for future growth. Composting can be made easier by adding worms or bacterial starters to help it break down faster. A good book on composting is *Let It Rot!* by Stu Campbell.

Intention

As we think, so it is. Benjamin Franklin once said that he saw "more people get ill from what came out of their mouths than from what went in." This is to say that we are what we think and say as much as, if not more than, we are what we eat. Some of the most unhealthy food a person can eat is food made by angry chefs or people who are upset. Love and positive intent can influence our creations as much as negativity and anger. By keeping a positive attitude while preparing food, we can add to the joy and experience people get when they eat.

Recipes

Food can be art. The best chefs are artists of visual appeal as well as flavor and texture. Once you know how to use the tools and what foods work with each other, you can create dazzling dishes to delight the eyes and mouth. All it takes is a little self-expression. These recipes are some fantastic discoveries that I made along the way. Remember to use your head, act with your heart, and follow your tongue.

Fruit Dishes

Star Fruit and Raspberry-Nut Kreme

Star fruit, also known as carambola, *has five to seven deep, lengthwise ribs that form beautiful star shapes when the fruit is sliced crosswise. The edges (points of the star) can be tougher than the rest of the fruit. It is often nice to remove the edges and the seeds before use.*

SERVES 2 TO 4

1 cup dates, seeded

1 cup filtered water

1 cup sprouted nuts (see page 44)

10 raspberries

2 ripe star fruits, thickly sliced crosswise

Fresh mint leaves, for garnish

Place the dates in a small bowl, cover with the water, and soak for about 1 hour, or until soft. Drain, reserving the liquid. Combine the dates, nuts, and raspberries in a blender. While blending slowly, add the reserved liquid as needed until the mixture becomes smooth. Arrange the star fruit on a plate. Spoon some of the nut kreme on each slice. Garnish with the mint leaves.

Fruit Rawies

These delicious dehydrator delights are quick and easy to make. These were originally called "fruit cookies" but since there is no cooking involved, I've dubbed them "rawies."

MAKES 12 TO 18 COOKIES

10 seeded, soaked dates (see page 42), drained

6 bananas, peeled and halved crosswise

1 cup peeled, cored, and coarsely chopped pineapple; or 4 apples, peeled, plus 1 cup walnuts; or 2 papayas, peeled and seeded

1 teaspoon ground cinnamon

Dash of vanilla

In a food processor, blend the dates, bananas, pineapple, cinnamon, and vanilla until the fruit is just slightly chunky. Form the mixture into little balls (2 to 3 tablespoons each) and flatten them until 1 inch thick on drying trays. Using one of the methods described on page 45, dehydrate for 18 hours, or until dry.

Tropical Fruit Salad

Tropical fruits can provide delicious new realms of flavor as well as varied forms of nutrition to your diet. Many of the tropical fruits in this salad can be obtained in Asian markets. If you live in the tropics, remove the seeds from the papayas, persimmons, and cherimoya, and plant them. In time, you'll be able to harvest and enjoy your own fruit.

SERVES 4

2 ripe papayas, peeled, seeded, and cut into 1/2-inch cubes

2 ripe mangos, peeled, seeded, and cut into 1/2-inch cubes

1 ripe pineapple, peeled and cut into 1/2-inch cubes

3 ripe Hachiya persimmons, seeded and cut into 1/2-inch cubes

1 ripe cherimoya, peeled, seeded, and cut into 1/2-inch cubes

1 small bunch ripe bananas, peeled and thickly sliced crosswise

1 ripe star fruit, peeled and thinly sliced crosswise

1 ripe kiwi, peeled and thinly sliced

Freshly shredded coconut, for garnish

Place the papayas, mangos, pineapple, persimmons, cherimoya, and bananas in a large serving bowl. Alternate star fruit and kiwi slices in a spiral over the top. Garnish with the shredded coconut.

Mixed Melon Ball Salad

This dish is entertaining due to its shapes and colors as well as its delicious flavors.

SERVES 2 TO 4

1 ripe cantaloupe, halved and seeded

1 ripe honeydew melon, halved and seeded

1 ripe watermelon, halved

Juice of 2 limes

Scoop out the flesh of the melons with a melon baller and place in a large serving bowl. Mix gently. Splash with the lime juice and serve.

Papaya Fundae

These "fundaes" are a great party dish and have always been one of the most popular desserts at our restaurants.

SERVES 2 TO 4

Carob Sauce

6 dates, seeded

¾ cup filtered water

2 tablespoons olive oil or hemp-seed oil

¼ cup raw carob powder

Black Raspberry Kreme

5 dates, seeded

½ cup filtered water

1 cup soaked cashews (see page 44)

⅓ cup black raspberries

8 ripe medium bananas, peeled and thickly sliced

2 ripe papayas, halved and seeded

Chopped walnuts, for garnish

To prepare the sauce, place the dates in a small bowl, cover with the water, and soak for about 1 hour, or until soft. Drain, reserving the liquid. In a food processor, combine the dates and the oil, slowly adding the reserved liquid as needed until the mixture is smooth. Add the carob powder and pulse until combined.

To make the raspberry kreme, place the dates in a small bowl and cover with the water, and soak for about 1 hour, or until soft. Drain, reserving the liquid. Place the dates, cashews, and black raspberries in a blender cup or blender, and while blending, add the reserved liquid as needed, until smooth.

Put the frozen bananas through a homogenizing juicer with a blank plate in place, or purée in a food processor until smooth. Fill the papaya halves with the pureed bananas, dividing equally. Top with 3 heaping tablespoons of the raspberry kreme. Drizzle the carob sauce over the papayas and raspberry kreme and garnish with the chopped walnuts.

Apples with Ginger Chutney

Apples are available year-round and make excellent "chips." By thinly slicing the apple lengthwise around the core, you can obtain an average of ten slices per apple.

SERVES 2 TO 4

10 dates, seeded

¾ cup filtered water

1½-inch piece fresh ginger

¼ cup freshly squeezed
  orange juice

Pinch of ground cinnamon

4 crisp apples, thinly sliced

Place the dates in a small bowl, cover with the water, and soak for about 1 hour, or until soft. Finely grate the ginger with a ginger grater or fine grater to extract its juice (you should have about 1 tablespoon). In a blender, combine the dates and their soaking water along with the ginger and orange juices and cinnamon. Blend until smooth. Arrange the apple slices on a plate and pour the date mixture over them, or serve the date mixture in a bowl with the apple slices around it.

Banana-Date Pudding

This dish was originally inspired by a banana-date-tofu pudding at an Asian vegetarian restaurant in New York City that made. I never did get the recipe for it, but this creation is an amazingly close raw version.

SERVES 2 TO 4

6 dates, seeded

½ cup filtered water

Seeds from ¼ of a split
  vanilla bean

6 ripe bananas, peeled
  and halved crosswise

Chopped walnuts, for garnish

Place the dates in a small bowl, cover with the water, and soak for about 1 hour, or until soft. In a food processor, blend the dates, their soaking water, and the vanilla seeds until smooth. Add the bananas and process until smooth. Spoon the pudding into individual serving bowls. Cover and refrigerate for 2 hours, or until chilled. Garnish with the chopped walnuts and serve.

Persimmon Sunburst

Hachiya persimmons, also known as Japanese persimmons, are very high in tannic acid when underripe and taste like very bitter chalk. To avoid this, make certain that your persimmons are fully ripe and soft. The skin should peel off the fruit easily if totally ripe.

SERVES 2 TO 4

6 dates, seeded
½ cup filtered water
½ cup fresh blueberries
4 ripe Hachiya persimmons

Place the dates in a small bowl, cover with the water, and soak for about 1 hour, or until soft. In a food processor, combine the dates, their soaking water, and the blueberries and process until smooth.

Starting at the point of each persimmon, slice an X shape through the skin, cutting all the way down to the nub on top. Place the fruit, point up, on serving plates. Gently peel the skin away from each fruit, and leave it hanging like the petals of a flower. Using a melon baller or a small spoon, scoop out a piece of each persimmon from the top of the open fruit. Spoon some of the blueberry sauce into the open persimmon points and drizzle more over the tops.

Applesauce

Applesauce is a great treat for kids and a quick and easy side dish. As a variation, add 1½ teaspoons of fresh ginger juice.

SERVES 2 TO 4

¼ cup raisins
¾ cup filtered water
Juice of ½ lemon
2 large, crisp apples, peeled and diced
Ground cinnamon, for garnish
Ground nutmeg, for garnish

Place the raisins in a small bowl, cover with the water, and soak for 1 hour. In a blender, combine the raisins, their soaking water, and the lemon juice and blend until smooth. Add the apples and blend until smooth. Sprinkle each serving with cinnamon and nutmeg.

Cherimoya Freeze

People throughout the South Pacific adore this dish. Many people in the Hawaiian Islands have told me it reminds them of childhood visits to local fruit stands where they'd enjoy a similar sticky, sweet frozen treat. When it is cherimoya season, I always make extra and fill my freezer. Serve with Buckies (page 176), chopped nuts, or on its own.

SERVES 2 TO 4

5 ripe cherimoyas, peeled and seeded

Juice of 2 limes

Put the cherimoyas in a sealed container and freeze about 8 hours, or until firm. Put the frozen fruit through a homogenizing juicer with the blank plate in place, or purée in a food processor until smooth. Add the lime juice and process until smooth. Pour into individual serving bowls and serve.

Banalmond Bliss

This creamy treat is an evolution of banana ice cream. As a frozen treat, this dish is pure bliss. Enjoy with Buckies (page 176) as an alternative to chopped nuts.

SERVES 2 TO 4

8 bananas, peeled and sliced

¼ cup Almond Mylk (page 55)

2 tablespoons raw almond butter

1 teaspoon vanilla extract

Chopped walnuts, for garnish (optional)

Place the bananas in a sealed container and freeze for 8 hours, until firm. Put the frozen bananas through a homogenizing juicer with the blank plate in place, or purée in a food processor until smooth. In a large bowl, combine the mylk, almond butter, and vanilla. Add the frozen banana purée and stir until combined. Freeze, covered, for 1 hour, or until firm. Transfer to individual serving bowls, garnish with the walnuts, and serve.

Pineapple-Pepper Salad

Peppers give this recipe just the right crunch. Apple mint adds an especially nice flavor to this salad, but if you can't find it, any sort of fresh mint will do.

SERVES 2 TO 4

1 large pineapple

2 red bell peppers, seeded and diced

4 kiwis, peeled and thinly sliced crosswise

¼ cup minced flat-leaf parsley

¼ cup minced apple mint leaves

Juice of ½ orange

With a sharp knife, carefully cut the pineapple in half lengthwise, remove and discard the core, and cut out the fruit, leaving 4 pineapple "boats." Remove the abrasive, brown eyes from the fruit. Dice the pineapple fruit.

In a large bowl mix together the diced pineapple, peppers, kiwis, and herbs. Stir in the orange juice. To serve, divide the salad among the empty pineapple halves.

Pineapple-Ginger Pudding

Pineapples are the highest source of bromelain, an enzyme that breaks down protein. They are so high in these enzymes that they can be used as a digestive stimulant that helps ease gastric issues and aids digestion.

SERVES 2 TO 4

10 dates, seeded

¾ cup filtered water

¾-inch piece fresh ginger

4 cups chopped, peeled pineapple

1 cup freshly squeezed lemon juice

Grated zest of 1 lemon

Coarsely ground almonds, for garnish

Place the dates in a small bowl, cover with the water, and soak for about 1 hour, or until soft. Drain, reserving the liquid. Finely grate the ginger with a ginger grater or fine grater to extract its juice (you should have 1½ teaspoons). Place the pineapple, lemon juice, zest, and ginger juice in a blender. Blend slowly, adding the reserved liquid as needed until smooth yet thick. Pour the pudding into a decorative bowl, sprinkle grated almonds over top, and serve.

Exotic Fruit Salad

Nature provides such a wide range of flavors and colors, and each area of the world has its own unique offerings. Travelers can take in more than just the sights of a foreign land; they can experience new tastes that broaden the senses. At home, look for tropical fruits in local Mexican or Asian markets. For a fun presentation of this salad, serve it in papaya boats—halved papayas with seeds and flesh removed.

SERVES 2 TO 4

2 cherimoyas, peeled, seeded, and sliced

1 papaya, peeled, seeded, and diced

1 mango, peeled, seeded, and diced

1 eggfruit *(canistel)*, peeled, seeded, and thinly sliced lengthwise

1 sapote, pulp seeded and mashed

5 to 10 Surinam *(pitanga)* cherries, pitted, or poha berries

Freshly shredded coconut, for garnish

Combine the cherimoya, papaya, mango, eggfruit, and sapote in a large serving bowl. Gently fold in the cherries. Sprinkle the shredded coconut on top and serve.

Mango Pudding

Mangos are among the most popular fruits in the world, and there are over three hundred varieties. The fruit's avid fans have cultivated it all over the world, and people still breed new strains today.

SERVES 2 TO 4

4 dates, seeded

½ cup filtered water

4 ripe mangos, peeled, seeded, and quartered

4 ripe bananas, peeled and halved crosswise

Freshly shredded coconut, for garnish

Place the dates in small bowl, cover with the water, and soak for about 1 hour, or until soft. Drain, reserving the liquid. In a blender, combine the mangos, bananas, dates, and ¼ cup of the reserved liquid and purée. If needed, add additional reserved liquid until the mixture is smooth yet thick. Transfer to a serving bowl and refrigerate 2 hours, or until well chilled. Garnish with the shredded coconut and serve.

Apple-Cinnamon Cup

This dish was inspired by harosset, *a traditional dish made of apples, walnuts, and wine eaten at Passover. Whenever I go to a Passover seder, I bring this dish, and it's always a big hit.*

SERVES 2 TO 4

6 seeded, soaked dates (see page 42), drained

Juice of ½ lemon

1 teaspoon ground cinnamon

1 teaspoon ground allspice

1 teaspoon freshly ground nutmeg

5 crisp apples (such as Fujis or Galas), shredded or cut into matchstick-sized pieces

¼ cup soaked raisins (see page 42), drained

2 tablespoons chopped walnuts, for garnish

In a food processor, combine the dates, lemon juice, cinnamon, allspice, and nutmeg and process until smooth. Transfer to a large bowl and stir in the apples and the raisins. Spoon the apple mixture into individual bowls or ramekins, garnish with the chopped walnuts, and serve.

Fabulous Fig Parfaits

Fresh figs are a wealth of life-force, containing thousands of tiny seeds that make them a very virile and hormone-rich food. These delicate fruits are very popular in the cuisines of Europe and the Middle East, where they originated. Feel free to use any sprouted nut in the preparation of the nut kreme; pecans are just my favorite.

SERVES 2 TO 4

½ cup dates, seeded

½ cup filtered water, plus additional as needed

Nut Kreme

½ cup sprouted pecans (see page 44)

Raspberry Sauce

¼ cup raspberries

8 fresh figs

Mint leaves or freshly shredded coconut, for garnish

Place the dates in a small bowl, cover with the ½ cup water, and soak for about 1 hour, or until soft. Drain, reserving the liquid.

To make the nut kreme, in a blender, purée the sprouted nuts and half of the dates, slowly adding up to ¼ cup of the reserved soaking liquid, until the mixture is smooth yet thick.

To make the raspberry sauce, blend the remaining half of the dates, the raspberries, and the remaining ¼ cup of the reserved liquid until smooth. The sauce should have a thin consistency; if needed, add additional filtered water.

To prepare the parfaits, starting from the top, cut the figs lengthwise into quarters (leaving the bottoms intact), and gently press open. Spoon some of the nut kreme into the middle of each fig. Arrange the parfaits on a platter and drizzle raspberry sauce over the top of each parfait. Garnish with the fresh mint leaves or shredded coconut.

Cinnamon-Apple Sprouted Wheat

Sprouted wheat, a fantastic source of protein, still contains some gluten. It can be replaced here with sprouted buckwheat, which is gluten free and even higher in protein.

SERVES 2 TO 4

8 seeded, soaked dates (see page 42), drained

2 cups sprouted wheat berries (see page 44)

2 apples, shredded

1 teaspoon ground cinnamon

1 teaspoon ground nutmeg

½ cup raisins, for garnish

Place the dates, wheat berries, apples, cinnamon, and nutmeg in a food processor and pulse until combined but still chunky. Transfer to a bowl, garnish with the raisins, and serve.

Mango Bliss

This recipe has provided joy and fun for everyone who has tried it. I find that simplicity is often best. Besides who could improve upon the mango?

DELIGHTS 1

Mango tree
Ladder (optional)

Pick a ripe mango from the tree. Peel and eat it immediately (preferably on the beach or near a river).

Bliss.
Swim.
Wow.

Fruit Soups

Ginger-Pear Soup

The pear makes this soup—so be sure to pick a good one. When selecting pears for this dish, it is best to use softer ones that are very ripe. I like to remove the skin before making this recipe as it yields a smoother consistency. To peel a ripe pear, just hold it under running water and rub the skin right off.

SERVES 2 TO 4

6 dates, seeded

2 cups filtered water

¼-inch piece fresh ginger

4 ripe pears such as Bartlett, peeled

½ teaspoon cinnamon

2 fresh anise flowers, or ½ teaspoon anise seeds, or a few wisps of Florence fennel

2 mint leaves

Black and white sesame seeds, for garnish

Place the dates in a small bowl, cover with the water, and soak for about 1 hour, or until soft. Drain, reserving the liquid. Finely grate the ginger with a ginger grater or fine grater to extract its juice (you should have ½ teaspoon). Place the dates, pears, cinnamon, anise, mint, and ginger juice in a blender. Slowly add the reserved liquid as needed while blending, until smooth. Pour into bowls. Garnish with the black and white sesame seeds.

Peach-Melon Soup

I had always been told that melons should either be eaten alone or left alone. In making melon soups, I've found that melons actually combine quite well with other foods—providing great taste and ease of digestion.

SERVES 2

1 large cantaloupe, halved and seeded

2 peaches, pitted

1½ cups freshly squeezed orange juice

½ teaspoon ground nutmeg

Using a metal spoon, scoop out the cantaloupe flesh, reserving half of the fruit for another use. Set aside both cantaloupe bowls. Place the remaining half of the cataloupe flesh, peaches, orange juice, and nutmeg in a blender. Blend until smooth. Divide the soup between the reserved cantaloupe bowls and serve.

Fennel-Berry Soup

In Kula, on the island of Maui, the Kula black raspberry grows. Wherever the raspberry grows, wild fennel grows as well. I would often rub my fingers on the fennel flowers and then pick the berries. The taste was fabulous and that is how the flavor combination for this soup was created.

SERVES 2 TO 4

3 cups raspberries

3 cups blueberries

2 tablespoons chopped fresh fennel leaves

2 cups filtered water

1 ripe avocado, pitted and peeled

Fresh fennel leaves, for garnish

Place the berries in a blender with the fennel. Blend while slowly adding the water. Add the avocado and continue to blend until smooth. Pour into bowls, garnish with the fennel leaves, and serve.

Watermelon Soup

A few years ago someone taught me a new technique for testing the ripeness of a watermelon: Set the watermelon on a table as it would sit on the ground. Take a dry straw from a broom, or a piece of hay, and lay it across the watermelon crosswise. The piece of straw will turn on its own toward the length of the watermelon. The more it turns, the riper the watermelon.

SERVES 2 TO 4

8 cups peeled, chopped, and seeded watermelon, juices reserved

Juice of 1 lime

Filtered water, as needed

Place the watermelon in a sealable plastic container or plastic bag and freeze for about 3 hours, or until very cold but not frozen. Transfer the watermelon to a blender; add the lime juice and the reserved watermelon juice and blend until thin but still chunky. If needed, add the water, ¼ cup at a time, until the correct consistency is reached. Transfer to a pitcher and freeze until well chilled, about 1 hour. Pour into bowls and serve.

Berry Soup

Any berry will work for this recipe. Blueberries are high in pectin and will produce a thicker soup, especially if left to set in the fridge for an hour. Raspberries and strawberries create a tangier, lighter soup.

SERVES 2 TO 4

4 cups berries (such as blueberries, strawberries, or raspberries)

8 seeded, soaked dates (see page 42), drained

1½ cups freshly squeezed orange juice

Place the berries and the dates in a food processor. While slowly adding the orange juice, blend until smooth. Cover and refrigerate until chilled, about 1 hour. Pour into bowls and serve.

Nectarine-Cardamom Soup

With its cardamom and cashews, this summertime delight has an East Indian flair.

SERVES 2 TO 4

4 nectarines, pitted

2 teaspoons ground cardamom

½ cup soaked cashews (see page 42), drained

1½ cups filtered water

Pinch of black sesame seeds

Place the nectarines, cardamom, cashews, and water in a blender. Blend until smooth. Pour into bowls, garnish with black sesame seeds, and serve.

Spicy Papaya-Lime Soup

Most of the papayas you'll find in the market today are hermaphrodites (half male, half female). These fruits are oblong and with a slight pear shape as opposed to the true female papayas which are round and have five lobes. I prefer the flavor of the true female papayas, but either kind will work fine in this dish.

SERVES 2 TO 4

2 papayas, peeled and seeded
Juice of 1 lime
Filtered water, as needed
Pinch of cayenne pepper

Place the papaya and the lime juice in a blender. Blend until the consistency is smooth. Add a little water, if needed, to thin. Pour into bowls, sprinkle each serving with cayenne, and serve.

Tropical Fruit Soup

This island-inspired soup has a delightful tropical flavor that will make you feel the aloha spirit.

SERVES 2 TO 4

½-inch piece fresh ginger
2 cups peeled, chopped
    pineapple
2 bananas, peeled and
    thickly sliced
2 papayas, peeled and seeded
1 cup coconut water or fresh
    pineapple juice
Pinch of beet powder
    (see page 37)

Finely grate the ginger on a ginger grater or fine greater to extract its juice (you should have 1 teaspoon). Place the pineapple, banana, papaya, and ginger juice in a blender. While slowly adding the coconut water, blend until smooth. Cover and refrigerate until chilled, about 1 to 2 hours. To serve, pour into bowls and sprinkle each serving with beet powder.

Persimmon Soup

Persimmons typically become ripe early in the fall, making it necessary to wait a whole year for this delicious soup. Luckily, in Hawaii there is a springtime fruit that is a close relative of the persimmon: the chocolate pudding fruit. Chocolate pudding fruit, also known as the chocolate persimmon or black sapote, works great for this soup, too.

SERVES 2 TO 4

5 ripe persimmons, peeled and chopped

Pinch of ground cinnamon

1 cup filtered water

Place the persimmons, cinnamon, and water in a blender and blend until smooth. Pour into bowls and enjoy.

Apple-Almond Soup

This is a classic combo. It tastes like apple pie in a bowl. If time allows, try sprouting the almonds as it makes for a less oily soup.

SERVES 2 TO 4

2 apples, cored

1/2 cup soaked or sprouted almonds (see page 42 or 44), drained

1 1/2 cups filtered water

1 teaspoon ground cinnamon

Place the apples and almonds in a blender. While slowly adding the water, blend until smooth. Pour into bowls and sprinkle each serving with cinnamon.

Drinks

Banana Mylk

In Hawaii, banana trees grow everywhere; from seed, it takes only nine months to get a hundred-pound stalk of bananas. Bananas are excellent for making mylk as they provide a creamy texture and a sweet yet subtle flavor. There are hundreds of varieties of banana, but Williams and Bluefield work the best. As a flavoring variation, try any of the following: blend in 2 tablespoons raw carob powder; blend in the seeds of half a vanilla bean; blend in the seeds of half a vanilla bean and 2 tablespoons raw cacao. You can also first freeze the bananas and enjoy a banana mylk shake with or without any of the above variations.

SERVES 2 TO 4

4 dates, seeded

1 cup filtered water, plus additional as needed

4 ripe bananas, peeled

Place the dates in a small bowl, cover with 1 cup of the water, and soak for about 1 hour, or until soft. Transfer the dates and their soaking water to a food processor and blend until smooth. Add the bananas and blend until creamy. The consistency should be creamy. If needed, add a little more water and pulse a few times until combined. Serve in a tall glass.

Banacado

One day while traveling the road to Hana, on Maui, I had the pleasure of harvesting both a ripe stalk of bananas and some ripe avocados. Being hungry after a long drive, I began munching on the bananas when I noticed that one of the avocados had gotten squished. I started eating the mashed avocado along with the banana and discovered a delicious new combination. Later I found out that the banana-avocado combination is a Hawaiian tradition.

SERVES 1 TO 2

2 dates, seeded

2 cups filtered water

4 ripe bananas, peeled and thickly sliced

1/2 ripe avocado, peeled and pitted

Place the dates in a small bowl, cover with the water, and soak for about 1 hour, or until soft. Drain, reserving the liquid. Place the bananas, avocado, and the reserved liquid in a blender and blend until combined. Add the dates and continue blending until a thick, smooth consistency is achieved. Serve in a tall glass.

Almond Mylk

I never really understood the concept of humans drinking milk from a cow. Cow's milk is designed to take an eighty-pound calf and turn it into a three-hundred-pound heifer in a few months. Almond Mylk has more nutrition than cow's milk and is far more absorbable into the human body. Sprouted almonds are also a great source of protein and amino acids.

SERVES 1 TO 2

3 dates, seeded

3 cups filtered water

½ cup sprouted almonds
(see page 44)

Place the dates in a bowl, cover with the water, and soak for about 1 hour, or until soft. Transfer the dates and their soaking water to a blender, add the almonds, and blend until smooth. Strain through a wire-mesh strainer into a tall glass and serve. (The pulp can be blended again for a lighter batch or used for "rawies," or dehydrated cookies.)

Cashew Mylk

This sweet and rich nut mylk is one of the most delicious and filling treats. Cashews blend up better than any other nut, so if you are looking for a really creamy consistency, use cashews. As a variation, blend in the seeds of half a vanilla bean or 3 tablespoons of raw carob powder along with the dates and nuts.

SERVES 1 TO 2

2 dates, seeded

½ cup cashews

3 cups filtered water

Place the dates and cashews in a small bowl, cover with water, and soak for about 1 hour, or until soft. Drain. Place the dates, the nuts, and the water in a blender and blend until creamy. Pour into a tall glass and enjoy.

Banalmond Mylk

This power-packed drink is great for providing extra energy. It's a favorite of a body-building couple I know. They say it goes right to their muscles. As a variation, blend in 2 teaspoons of raw carob powder.

SERVES 1 TO 2

4 dates, seeded

2½ cups filtered water

½ cup sprouted almonds (see page 44)

½ vanilla bean

4 bananas, peeled, frozen, and thickly sliced

Place the dates in a small bowl, cover with ½ cup of the water, and soak for about 1 hour, or until soft. Place the sprouted almonds and the remaining 2 cups of water in a blender, and blend until smooth. Strain through a wire-mesh strainer, discarding the almond pulp. Return the almond mylk to the blender, add the dates, along with their soaking water, and the vanilla bean. Blend until smooth. Add the bananas, and blend again until smooth. Serve in tall glasses.

Rejuvelac

Dr. Ann Wigmore, the woman who brought sprouts and wheatgrass to the world, was a major proponent of rejuvelac, a cultured-grain drink full of healthy bacteria and enzymes helpful in the digestion of raw food (particularly when transitioning to a raw-food diet). Drinking rejuvelac is also an excellent way to bring positive flora into the intestinal tract, thereby bringing the body into a more alkaline balance and strengthening the immune system.

SERVES 2 TO 4

1 cup sprouted wheat berries or sprouted quinoa (see page 44), with sprouts of equal length as the seed

7 cups filtered water

Place the sprouts in a clean ½-gallon jug and add the water. Cover with a screen or leave open. Place the jug in a warm area out of direct sunlight, and soak the sprouts overnight. Strain through a wire-mesh strainer, discarding the soaked wheat berries. The rejuvelac should smell slightly sour. Refrigerate until chilled before serving.

Freedom's Froth

When I first used to visit the Hawaiian Islands I would stay with Freedom, who lives in the jungle of Maui. The Raw Experience was born out of some ideas that Freedom and I had tossed around during those visits. He never got involved in the restaurant, but this drink was a permanent feature on the menu as a tribute to him and his favorite smoothie.

SERVES 1 TO 2

2 ripe papayas, peeled and seeded

4 bananas, peeled, frozen, and thickly sliced

Juice of 2 small limes

1 to 2 cups coconut water or filtered water

Place the papayas, bananas, lime juice, and 1 cup of the coconut water in a blender and blend until combined. While continuing to blend, slowly add up to 1 cup of the remaining coconut water until smooth and thick.

Tangy Tango

Kiwis are also known as Chinese gooseberries. There is actually a miniature strain of kiwis and a golden kiwi. All of them work great in this tasty and tangy smoothie.

SERVES 1 TO 2

1 large, ripe papaya, peeled and seeded

1/2 cup raspberries

1 ripe kiwi, peeled and coarsely chopped

Juice of 1 large lime

4 frozen bananas, peeled, frozen, and thickly sliced

1 1/2 cups filtered water

Place all of the ingredients in a blender and blend until smooth. Pour into a tall glass and serve.

Tropical Ambrosia

This piña colada–style smoothie is a delicious tropical drink. Pineapples are propagated by planting the top crown. A few years later a new pineapple grows out the center of the crown of the old one.

SERVES 1 TO 2

1 pineapple, peeled and cored

1 cup fresh, finely chopped coconut meat

4 bananas, peeled, frozen, and thickly sliced

Place the pineapple in a juice press or juicer and juice. You should have about 2 cups of pineapple juice. Reserve the pineapple flesh for making Fruit Rawies (page 50). Place the pineapple juice, coconut, and bananas in a blender and blend until smooth. Serve in tall glasses.

Banaberry

This is your standard smoothie. All I can say is it is berry good.

SERVES 1 TO 2

½ cup raspberries

½ cup hulled strawberries

½ cup blueberries

2 bananas, peeled, frozen, and thickly sliced

1 to 2 cups fresh apple juice (2 to 4 apples) or filtered water

Place the raspberries, strawberries, blueberries, and bananas in a blender. While slowly adding at least 1 cup and up to 2 cups of the apple juice, as needed, blend until smooth.

Nature's Nectar

This smoothie tastes like coconut cream pie.

SERVES 1 TO 2

3 dates, seeded

2 cups filtered water

1 cup freshly shredded coconut

Place the dates in a small bowl, cover with the water, and soak for about 1 hour, or until soft. Transfer the dates and their soaking water to a blender, add the coconut, and blend until smooth. Pour into a glass and serve.

Coconut Milk

Coconuts have the bad reputation of being high in fat, but coconut water contains no fat and coconut meat, depending on its maturity, can contain lots of healthy, good fats. It is amazing how much misinformation is out there.

MAKES 1½ CUPS

½ cup fresh coconut meat
1 cup coconut water

Place both ingredients in a blender and blend until smooth. Strain.

Storange Smooth

This is a vitamin C–packed smoothie. Many people think of oranges as a great source of vitamin C. Although oranges do contain a fair amount of the vitamin, the top honors go to acerola cherries, hot chile peppers, and strawberries.

SERVES 1 TO 2

½ cup hulled strawberries
2 cups freshly squeezed orange juice
2 bananas, peeled, frozen, and thickly sliced

Place all of the ingredients in blender and blend until smooth. Serve in a tall glass.

Fruit Root

Apples and carrots both are harvested in abundance in the fall. Combining the fruit of the tree and the root of the earth creates a tasty and well-balanced drink—the best of the earth and sky.

SERVES 1 TO 2

6 apples, seeded
6 carrots

Process both ingredients through a juicer into a bowl. Pour into glasses and serve.

Lilistar

Star fruit, or carambola, are a sweet juicy fruit with a very mild flavor. Mixing it with the juice of the passion fruit (lilikoi), *brings out the tropical tang.*

SERVES 2 TO 4

5 star fruits, ribs removed
   and seeded
1 passion fruit, shell removed

Process the fruits through a juicer or purée in a blender and strain. Pour into glasses and serve.

Soursop-Pineapple

The soursop, or guanabana, is a spiky cousin of the cherimoya. Soursop skins are usually green but if the soursop is allowed to fully mature in the tropics, it turns silver. Make certain to remove all soursop seeds since they are poisonous.

SERVES 2 TO 4

1 soursop, peeled and seeded
1 pineapple, peeled, cored, and
   chopped

Process the fruit through a juicer into a bowl, pour into glasses, and enjoy.

Apple Zing

This zippy drink is a delight to the taste buds. It is nice to juice the rind of the lemon through the juicer for an added spark of flavor.

SERVES 1 TO 2

10 apples, seeded
½-inch piece fresh ginger
⅓ of a lemon with rind, or juice
   of 1 lemon

Process the apples and ginger through a juicer into a bowl. Juice the lemon with rind, or stir in the lemon juice once the apples and ginger have been juiced. Pour into glasses and enjoy.

Green Dream

Spirulina, an ocean algae, is the highest source of protein on the planet. I talk to people all the time who ask me where to get protein in a vegetarian diet. I always tell them that beef is about 25 percent protein; milk, 30 percent; soy beans, 35 percent; and spirulina, a whopping 70 percent protein! Besides its fabulous protein content, spirulina contains every vitamin and mineral. That's a lot of nutrition for one of the simplest single-celled life forms on earth.

SERVES 1 TO 2

4 dates, seeded

1½ cups filtered water

2 ripe papayas, peeled and seeded

1 cup coconut water

4 bananas, peeled, frozen, and thickly sliced

1 to 2 tablespoons spirulina powder

Place the dates in a small bowl, cover with the water, and soak for about 1 hour, or until soft. Transfer the dates and their soaking water to a blender, and blend until smooth. Add the papayas and the coconut water and blend to combine. Add the frozen bananas and the spirulina and blend until smooth. Pour into a tall glass.

Sunshine

This bright orange smoothie is a delight to the eyes as well as the taste buds. For a pumpkin pie–flavored variation, add pinches of ground cinnamon, nutmeg, and clove.

SERVES 2 TO 4

7 apples, seeded, or filtered water

4 ripe persimmons, peeled and seeded

2 bananas, peeled, frozen, and thickly sliced

Process the apples through a juicer into a large measuring cup (you should have about 2 cups). Place the persimmons and 1 cup of the apple juice in a blender, and blend until smooth. Add the bananas and blend until smooth and creamy, adding the additional apple juice if needed.

Thin Mint

This smoothie was inspired by everyone's favorite Girl Scout cookie, and it's as tasty as its namesake. For a different treat you can dehydrate this smoothie into rawies.

SERVES 1 TO 2

6 dates, seeded

1½ cups filtered water

1 large sprig fresh mint

3 tablespoons raw carob powder

1 cup coconut milk (page 74)

4 bananas, peeled, frozen, and thickly sliced

Place the dates in a small bowl, cover with the water, and soak for about 1 hour, or until soft. Place the dates and their soaking water in a blender, add the mint and carob powder, and blend until smooth. Blend in the coconut milk and the bananas until smooth. Serve in a tall glass.

Complementary

The look of this delicious smoothie determined its name. When blended up, the drink's orange color is perfectly set off by the flecks of blue scattered throughout.

SERVES 2 TO 4

1 ripe mango, peeled and seeded

2 ripe peaches, peeled and pitted

½ cup blueberries

4 bananas, peeled, frozen, and thickly sliced

2 cups freshly squeezed orange juice or coconut water

Place all of the ingredients in blender and blend until smooth. Pour into tall glasses and serve.

Cream Dream

Cherimoya and banana in a smoothie is about as creamy as it gets. This white, frosty drink is as sweet as ice cream and just as silky.

SERVES 1 TO 2

7 apples, seeded, or filtered water

2 ripe cherimoyas, peeled and seeded

2 bananas, peeled, frozen, and thickly sliced

Juice of 1 lime (optional)

Process the apples through a juicer into a large measuring cup (you should have about 2 cups). Place the cherimoyas, bananas, 1 cup of the apple juice, and the lime juice in a blender and blend until smooth. Add additional apple juice if necessary to create a smooth, thick consistency. Pour into glasses and serve.

Green Clean

This green drink comes close to providing the nutrition and cleansing benefits of wheatgrass juice and is far tastier to drink.

SERVES 1 TO 2

2 to 3 leaves kale

3 stalks celery

1 cucumber

½ cup loosely packed parsley leaves

½ cup loosely packed watercress

Process all of the ingredients through a juicer into a bowl. Pour into glasses and serve.

Nut Bliss

This delightful combination of nut mylks and bananas makes for a thick, frozen shake reminiscent of an ice cream milk shake.

SERVES 2 TO 4

Seeds of ½ vanilla bean

¼ cup filtered water

1 cup Almond Mylk (page 55)

1 cup coconut milk (page 74)

4 bananas, peeled, frozen, and thickly sliced

4 seeded, soaked dates (see page 42), drained

Place the seeds and the water in a blender. Blend until smooth. Add the mylk and coconut milk and blend to combine. Add the frozen bananas and dates and blend until smooth. Pour into glasses and enjoy.

Flaxative

Flax seeds are a great source of fiber and can help to clean out the intestinal tract. This drink is a great way to help keep things moving.

SERVES 1 TO 2

¼ cup flax seeds

1 cup filtered water (optional)

4 apples, seeded

2 bananas, peeled, frozen, and thickly sliced

The flax seeds may be prepared in one of two ways: Place the flax seeds in a bowl, cover with the water, and soak for 15 minutes, until the seeds have absorbed all of the water and a gel is formed. Alternatively, grind the flax seeds into a powder using a coffee grinder or a small food processor. Process the apples through a juicer into a large measuring cup (you should have about 1½ cups). In a blender, blend the flax and apple juice until smooth. Add the bananas and blend again until smooth. Pour into a tall glass.

White Delight

The vanilla sapote is misnamed since it is actually not a member of the sapote family but a member of the citrus family. Vanilla sapotes, also called white sapotes, are green on the outside with pale, ivory flesh. The green sapote (a true sapote) is green on the outside and orange on the inside. Look for vanilla sapotes at Latin markets and specialty produce stores.

SERVES 2 TO 4

- 8 apples, seeded, or 3 cups filtered water
- 2 vanilla sapotes, seeded
- 1 large, ripe cherimoya, peeled and seeded
- 2 bananas, peeled, frozen, and cut into chunks
- 1/2 vanilla bean (optional)

Process the apples through a juicer into a large measuring cup (you should have about 3 cups). Place 2½ cups of the apple juice and the sapotes, cherimoya, bananas, and vanilla in a blender and blend until smooth, adding the additional ½ cup of apple juice if needed to create a soupy consistency.

Mellow Melon

There are many ways to juice a watermelon, but my preference is to use a juice press, which keeps the liquid vital and prevents oxidation for up to twenty-four hours. When the juice oxidizes, it separates and forms sedimentary particles. If you obtain the juice any other way (centrifuging, masticating, grinding), then the juice will oxidize in less than one hour. It is amazing to see a glass of freshly pressed watermelon juice—it glows brightly, especially when put in the sun.

SERVES 2 TO 4

- 1 huge, fresh watermelon (about 8 to 10 pounds), rind removed and chopped

Place the watermelon in a juice press or in a cloth bag over a bowl, and press or squeeze firmly. You can also blend the watermelon in a blender, slowly at first, then faster, and then strain. Pour into tall glasses and serve.

Fire Water

This is a great way to start a meal. Fire Water was served at the Raw Experience as a palate cleanser and digestive stimulant. It was a great opener to a meal at the Raw Experience and provided a new spin on stepping up to the bar and throwing down a shot.

SERVES 8 TO 16

2 quarts filtered water

3 chiles (such as habanero, jalapeño, or serrano, or a combination for added flavor), thinly sliced lengthwise

1 lemon, coarsely diced

Juice of 1 orange

2 teaspoons beet powder (see page 37)

Place all of the ingredients in a large glass jar with a lid. Cover, shake well, and refrigerate for at least 2 hours or overnight. Pour into shot glasses, being careful to leave the chiles in the jar, and serve.

Sweet Lime and Aloe

Aloe vera leaves are a powerful intestinal cleanser, but the flesh is extremely bitter and often a challenge to eat. Citrus juice makes aloe much more tasty. Look for cold-pressed aloe vera gel at health food stores.

SERVES 2 TO 4

1 cup filtered water

1 tablespoon cold-pressed aloe vera gel

Juice of ½ lime

2 cups freshly squeezed orange juice

Place all of the ingredients in a blender. Blend very thoroughly. Pour into glasses and serve.

Nut Shake

When using frozen bananas, slice them up before putting them in the blender. This will ensure that all of the pieces blend up evenly, resulting in the most creamy "milk shake" imaginable.

SERVES 1 TO 2

5 dates, seeded

2¾ cups filtered water

Seeds from ½ vanilla bean

½ cup sprouted almonds
(see page 44)

4 bananas, peeled, frozen,
and thickly sliced

Place the dates in a small bowl, cover with ¾ cup of the water, and soak for about 1 hour, or until soft. In a blender, blend the dates, along with their soaking water, and the vanilla seeds until smooth. Add the almonds and the remaining 2 cups of water and blend until smooth. Add the bananas and continue blending until smooth. Pour into glasses and serve.

Ruby Cooler (Sun Tea)

Sun tea uses concentrated sunlight to extract flavor and essence from herbs, fruits, and flowers. The pH of the water determines how fast it will extract the tea. The more alkaline the water, the faster it will extract the tea.

SERVES 2 TO 4

⅓ cup dried hibiscus leaves

⅓ cup dried rose hips

6 cups filtered water

½ cup freshly squeezed
lemon juice

1 cup freshly squeezed
orange juice

½ cup pineapple juice
(optional)

2 to 4 lemon or orange wedges,
for garnish

Place hibiscus leaves and rose hips in a large glass jar and cover with the water. Cover the top and set the jar in direct sunlight for 3 to 6 hours. Stir in the lemon, orange, and pineapple juices, and refrigerate until chilled, about 2 hours. Serve in tall glasses, garnished with a wedge of lemon or orange.

Black Raspberry–Prickly Pear

Prickly pears grow prolifically in Hawaii and in the Southwestern United States. Many native tribes subsisted primarily on the fruit for almost one third of the year, while it was in season. The prickly pear is covered with hundreds of tiny thorns, so when dealing with it, be careful! The barbed thorns are as small as fiberglass. Make certain to wipe down all cutting areas after preparing this fruit.

SERVES 2 TO 4

7 large prickly pears

10 black raspberries

1 cup filtered water or coconut water (optional)

To peel the prickly pears, make a ¼-inch-deep, lengthwise cut through the skins. Cut off both ends of the prickly pears, and peel back the skins, removing the fruit. Discard the skins. Juice the prickly pears along with the raspberries in a juicer or purée in a blender and strain. Transfer to a pitcher, add the water if a thinner consistency is desired, stir to combine, and enjoy!

Ginger Blast

Ginger grows wild in riverbeds and the jungles throughout Maui. While hiking in the woods, the smell of fresh ginger is everywhere. Its wonderful scent and flavor enhance this bracing drink.

SERVES 1 TO 2

1 pineapple, peeled and cored

2- to 3-inch piece fresh ginger, peeled and minced (about ¼ cup)

½ cup filtered water

Juice of 2 lemons

Process the pineapple through a juicer into a large measuring cup (you should have about 2 cups). In a blender, thoroughly blend the ginger with the water. Strain through a sieve, discarding the ginger solids. In a pitcher, stir together the pineapple juice and lemon juice. Add the ginger water and stir to combine. Chill before serving.

Liver Cleanse

This drink is a great way to care for your liver, which filters the blood and cleanses many of the toxins the body encounters. This drink helps the liver remove old waste and also helps clear the gall bladder. This drink was called the "Elvis Parsley" on the Raw Experience menu because it made you shimmy and shake.

SERVES 1 TO 2

¼ cup loosely packed parsley
 sprigs

1 clove garlic

2 cups freshly squeezed
 orange juice

Juice of 1 lemon

1 tablespoon olive or flax oil

Pinch of cayenne pepper

In a blender, blend the parsley, garlic, and 1 cup of the orange juice. Strain through a wire-mesh sieve into a pitcher. Add the remaining 1 cup of orange juice, the lemon juice, oil, and cayenne, and stir. Serve immediately.

eVe-8

This flavorful drink combines eight vegetables and is power-packed with a wide range of nutrients that provide long-lasting energy.

SERVES 1 TO 2

2 tomatoes

1 carrot

1 beet, peeled

1 yellow bell pepper

1 cucumber, ends trimmed
 and rubbed (see page 85)

2 stalks celery

½ cup loosely packed parsley
 leaves

1 to 2 cloves garlic

Shots of wheatgrass juice
 (optional)

Process the vegetables through a juicer into a bowl and stir to combine. Pour into glasses. Add a shot of wheatgrass to each glass for a lively kick!

Cooling Green

This light and juicy drink is satisfying and provides an abundance of minerals. Cucumbers contain much of their vital nutrients in their skin. Unfortunately, the flavor of a cucumber's skin is quite bitter. Remove this bitterness by following these simple instructions, and enjoy a far tastier cucumber—skin included: Cut the tips off of the cucumber. Take the tip from one end and rub its exposed flesh in small circles on the skin near the opposite end until a milky white sap comes out of the skin. Repeat, using the other tip on the skin of the opposite end. Cut off the new ends now coated in white sap and use your new, improved cucumber.

SERVES 1 TO 2

1 large cucumber
5 stalks celery
1 teaspoon powdered kelp

Process the cucumber and celery through a juicer into a bowl. Stir in the kelp. Pour into glasses and enjoy.

Intestinal Cleanse

Every once in a while it is a good idea to help clear the intestines. Many people eat far more than needed or could have eaten better foods in their youth and are now ready to cleanse the unhealthy remains from their systems. This drink is a sweet and easy way toward better health.

SERVES 1 TO 2

10 apples, seeded
Juice of 1 lemon
1 tablespoon psyllium husks

Process the apples through a juicer into a bowl (you should have about 4 cups). Blend or stir in the lemon and psyllium. Pour into glasses and serve.

Sprout Power

Sprouts contain some of the most abundant life force on the planet—they're the potential energy of a whole plant. When given the opportunity to sprout, a seed will spend as much energy as possible to get a root in the earth and a leaf up to heaven. In doing so, a sprout creates more concentrated nutrition per ounce than it ever will in its entire life. Grow your own sprouts, following the simple directions on page 45.

SERVES 1 TO 2

4 medium tomatoes, cored

1 cup loosely packed sunflower sprouts (see page 44)

½ cup alfalfa sprouts (see page 44)

Juice of ½ lemon

1 teaspoon powdered kelp

1 teaspoon nutritional yeast (optional)

Process the tomatoes and the sprouts through a juicer into a bowl. Stir in the lemon juice, kelp, and yeast. Pour into glasses and serve.

Iron Lion

This earthy root drink is made with a classic vegetable combo: carrots and beets. It is nice to do this one with dark red beets for a really earthy taste. Golden beets provide a far lighter flavor but are very nice in this drink, too. Beets are an excellent source of iron.

SERVES 1 TO 2

6 carrots

1 beet, peeled

½ cup loosely packed parsley leaves

Process the carrots, beet, and parsley through a juicer into glasses and serve.

Salads

Mixed Field Greens with Edible Flowers

Everywhere I go I find greens to eat. Wild greens grow without any cultivation or help. They have so much zest for life that they take over people's gardens. In the end they just get insulted by being called weeds. I say, "Eat the weeds!" This salad is eater's choice. Use what you like; some greens are spicy while other are bitter or sweet. Some edible flowers have a distinct flavor while others are just there for color (see page 16). Be creative and design a salad that suits your tastes and is made of greens found in your area. Consult the greens listed on page 21 for ideas.

SERVES: AN UNDETERMINED AMOUNT OF PEOPLE

Greens of your choice

Edible flowers, for garnish

Salad dressing of your choice
(see page 100), for drizzling

In a bowl, make a bed of the greens. Garnish with the flowers and drizzle the dressing over the salad.

Shredded Salad

Salads of shredded vegetables are a welcome side dish to any meal; they're quick to make and are highly filling.

SERVES 2 TO 4

3 carrots, shredded

2 purple potatoes, shredded and rinsed

2 beets, shredded

2 cups shredded cabbage (about 1/2 head)

2 cups Carrot-Cashew-Ginger Dressing (page 104)

In a salad bowl, toss together the carrots, potatoes, beets, and cabbage. Drizzle the dressing on top, and serve.

Garden Salad

This salad is standard fare in any restaurant. Nothing fancy, no frills, just your basic side salad. It's a quick and easy addition to a meal that just needs a little something extra. Make it with the freshest ingredients and it will be something special.

SERVES 2 TO 4

1 small head red leaf lettuce, torn into small pieces

1 small head green leaf lettuce, torn into small pieces

1 cup radish, clover, and sesame sprouts

1 cucumber, thinly sliced

2 large tomatoes, cored and cut into wedges

2 cups Green Goddess Dressing (see page 103)

2 carrots, shredded

Pansy flowers, for garnish

In a large bowl, make a bed of the lettuces and sprouts. Top with the cucumber and tomatoes and drizzle with the salad dressing. Garnish with the carrots and pansies.

Zucchini-Squash Salad

The curcurbits sometimes have a bitter taste to them. To improve their flavor considerably, soak the chopped zucchini and yellow squash in water with a pinch of salt and a dash of lemon juice, then rinse thoroughly.

SERVES 2 TO 4

2 zucchini, cubed

2 yellow squash, cubed

1 onion, diced

1 1/2 cups Almond-Cumin Dressing (page 108)

In a salad bowl, combine the zucchini, yellow squash, and onion. Drizzle the dressing on top, and serve.

Waldorf Salad

The Waldorf salad was a popular dish originally created for the Waldorf Hotel in New York City. This raw evolution of the traditional salad is tastier than the original and offers a unique flavor combination.

SERVES 2 TO 4

1 small Belgian endive, separated into leaves

1 large head red leaf lettuce

¼ cup peeled, shredded jicama

3 stalks celery, diced

1 apple, diced

1 cup sunflower sprouts (see page 44)

½ cup walnuts, chopped

1 cup red or green grapes

2 cups Waldorf Dressing (page 101)

Arrange the five nicest endive leaves into the shape of a star around the sides of a salad bowl. By hand, tear the lettuce leaves into small pieces, then slice the remaining endive leaves crosswise. Mix together the sliced endive leaves and the torn lettuce and add to the salad bowl. In another bowl, combine the jicama, celery, apple, and sprouts. Place the jicama mixture on top of the greens. Sprinkle the chopped walnuts on top of the jicama mixture and the greens, then arrange the grapes on top to form a ring. Finish by drizzling the salad with the dressing. Serve immediately.

Corn, Carrot, and Pea Salad

This salad evolved from a cooked dish using frozen corn, carrots, and peas that I remember eating at summer camp. When I finally got around to making it raw, I was amazed at how much better it was than the original. Machine-processed, frozen, thawed, and cooked vegetables just don't compare to their fresh, natural counterparts.

SERVES 2 TO 4

2 cups corn kernels (approximately 4 ears of corn)

4 carrots, shredded

1 cup peas removed from their pods (approximately 1 pound peas in their pods)

1 small onion, diced and rinsed

Combine all of the ingredients in a salad bowl. Toss and serve.

Deluxe Salad

This was the standard salad at the Raw Experience. Many of the restaurant's recipes changed over the years but this one stayed the same. If it ain't broke, don't fix it.

SERVES 2 TO 4

1 head romaine lettuce, torn into small pieces

1 head red oak lettuce, torn into small pieces

2 heaping tablespoons alfalfa sprouts

2 heaping tablespoons shredded carrot

2 heaping tablespoons shredded beet

½ avocado, peeled, pitted, and thinly sliced

2 tablespoons seeded, chopped bell pepper

2 cups Carrot-Cashew-Ginger Dressing (page 104)

In a large salad bowl, make a bed of the lettuces and sprouts. Top with the carrot, beet, avocado, and bell pepper. Drizzle the dressing on top and serve.

Cucumber-Jicama Salad

This cool and crisp salad is a great option when you want a lively texture. It has a great crunch to it and is fun to make.

SERVES 2 TO 4

1 cucumber, diced

1 jicama, peeled and diced

1 apple, diced

2 stalks celery, diced

2 cups Creamy Herb Dressing (page 102) or Cucumber-Dill Dressing (page 108)

Combine the cucumber, jicama, apple, and celery in a salad bowl and gently toss. Drizzle the dressing on top, and serve.

Sprout Salad

There is no substitute for growing your own food. Having a daily interaction with plants that ultimately provide you with food and nutrition is one of the greatest pleasures there is. Sprouts grow quickly and easily and can be grown in any season and in almost any situation (see page 45 for sprouting directions). I know people who grow sprouts while hiking, in their vehicle while traveling, as well as in their kitchen. This recipe is full of life force and packed with nutrients, and if you have grown the sprouts yourself, you can be certain that they will contain lots of your loving energy, too.

SERVES 2 TO 4

1 tablespoon flax seeds

¼ cup filtered water

2 cups sunflower greens (see page 44)

2 cups buckwheat greens (see page 44)

½ cup alfalfa sprouts

¼ cup wheat sprouts

2 tablespoons sunflower sprouts

2 tablespoons sesame sprouts

2 cups Green Goddess Dressing (page 103)

Place the flax seeds in a small bowl, cover with the water, and soak for 15 minutes, until the seeds have absorbed all of the water and a gel is formed. In a salad bowl, create a bed of the sunflower and buckwheat greens and alfalfa sprouts. Garnish with the wheat, sunflower and sesame seeds, and soaked flax seeds. Drizzle salad dressing over the salad and serve.

Little Italy Salad

This rich and aromatic salad—a classic from the Raw Experience kitchen—makes a hearty side dish you can also serve on a bed of greens and drizzle with Italian Dressing (page 107). Marinated portobello mushrooms and sun-dried tomatoes lend a meaty flavor. The tomatoes and black olives also give a nice color contrast.

SERVES 4

½ cup dry-packed sun-dried tomatoes (golden if available)

1 large portobello mushroom, stemmed and cut into ½-inch pieces

2 tablespoons Bragg Liquid Aminos

1 small clove garlic, pressed

2 to 5 basil leaves, coarsely chopped

2 oregano sprigs, coarsely chopped

Juice of ½ lemon

¼ cup olives, pitted and diced

2 tablespoons diced red bell pepper

2 tablespoons minced onions

2 tablespoons olive oil

Place the sun-dried tomatoes in a small bowl, cover with water, and soak for about 1 hour, or until soft. In another bowl, combine the portobello, Braggs, garlic, basil, oregano, and lemon juice. Cover and marinate for at least 1 hour. Drain the sun-dried tomatoes and slice them into small strips. In a separate, large bowl, combine the sun-dried tomatoes with the olives and bell pepper.

To keep their flavor from dominating, rinse the onions with water in a wire-mesh sieve. Drain the mushroom mixture, reserving the marinade for other uses. Add the onions and the mushrooms to the bowl containing the sun-dried tomatoes, add the olive oil, and stir to combine. If needed for additional flavor, add ¼ cup of the reserved marinade.

Green Papaya Salad

Island people all across the South Pacific, including Hawaii, eat green papaya salad. There are two things referred to as the green papaya: One is a long large papaya that doesn't ripen well and is only used green; the other is just a regular papaya that is used before it is ripe. Either may be used in this recipe. Green papaya has a much higher papain content than ripe papaya and therefore is even better as a digestive stimulant. Seeds of the green papaya, when dried and ground, make an excellent replacement for black pepper.

SERVES 4

2 green papayas, peeled and seeded

1 yellow bell pepper, seeded and diced

1 red bell pepper, seeded and diced

½ cup diced red onion, rinsed and drained

¼-inch piece fresh ginger

2 tablespoons minced fresh parsley

2 cloves garlic, pressed

1 fresh jalapeño, minced

2 tablespoons olive oil

2 tablespoons apple cider vinegar

3 tablespoons Bragg Liquid Aminos

Juice of 1 lemon

Juice of 1 lime

Shred the papaya using a hand shredder or the shredding blade of a food processor. In a large bowl, combine the papaya, yellow and red bell peppers, and onion. Finely grate the ginger on a ginger grate or fine grater to extract its juice (you should have about ½ teaspoon). Add to the papaya mixture along with the parsley, garlic, and jalapeño. Season with the olive oil, vinegar, Braggs, lemon juice, and lime juice.

Serve as a side dish or on bed of mixed greens with Spicy Papaya-Lime Dressing (page 102).

Greek Salad

From the salsas of Mexico to the tapenade of Italy, and even to the green papaya salad of the South Pacific, every culture has something to offer the world of raw-food cuisine. This salad borrows from Greece, whose cuisine features many traditional salads with cheese. This classic Greek salad utilizes seed cheese in place of dairy cheese, and olives, another Grecian food staple.

SERVES 4

1 head romaine lettuce

2 tomatoes, diced

2 cucumbers, diced

½ cup olives, pitted and diced

1 tablespoon minced fresh oregano

1 tablespoon minced fresh basil

1 tablespoon flax oil

1 tablespoon Bragg Liquid Aminos

1 tablespoon apple cider vinegar

Juice of 1 lemon

¼ cup Basic Seed Cheeze (page 144)

Tear the lettuce by hand and place in a large salad bowl. Add the tomatoes and cucumbers. In a separate bowl, mix the olives, oregano, basil, flax oil, Braggs, vinegar, and lemon juice. Add the olive mixture to the bowl containing the lettuce and toss. Serve with the seed cheeze on the side, or add the seed cheeze to the salad, toss lightly, and serve.

Sea Salad

This is a mineral-rich salad with an Asian flair. Sea vegetables such as seaweed are a wild, harvested food. They grow in oceans throughout the world. Ideally, get fresh sea vegetables that grow in your area (if you live by the sea); if not, then buy the dried ones. There are a wide number of seaweeds out there, so find one you like and read the packages well. Avoid sea veggies that are cooked before sun drying. Dried sea vegetables such as dulse, sea palm, and wakame are almost always dried fresh, while hijiki and arame are usually cooked first. Two good suppliers of raw sea vegetables are the Mendocino Sea Vegetable Company (www.seaweed.net) and Gold Mine Natural Food Co. (www.goldminenaturalfood.com).

SERVES 4

1 large red cabbage, shredded

1 large napa cabbage, shredded

3 large carrots, shredded

2 green onions, thinly sliced

2 cups wet seaweed, rinsed and coarsely chopped, or 1 cup dried seaweed, soaked, drained, and chopped

Heaping ¼ cup sesame seeds, white or black or a combination

1-inch piece fresh ginger

3 tablespoons Bragg Liquid Aminos

2 tablespoons rice wine vinegar or white wine vinegar or other vinegar

Juice of 1 lemon

Juice of 1 orange

In a large bowl, toss together the red and napa cabbages. Add the carrots, green onions, seaweed, and 3 tablespoons of the sesame seeds. Mix well. Finely grate the ginger on a ginger grater or fine grater to extract its juice (you should have about 2 teaspoons). Place in a small bowl, add the Braggs, vinegar, ginger juice, lemon juice, and orange juice, and stir to combine. Drizzle over the cabbage mixture and toss well. Garnish with the remaining sesame seeds.

Serve on its own or on a bed of greens with Miso-Tahini Dressing (page 106). For individual servings, serve the salad in a large red cabbage leaf.

Creamy Coleslaw

Coleslaw has always been one of the great American picnic foods. This version's creamy consistency—the result of a special balance between its acids and oils—and its flavor of vinegar, tahini, and dates together enhanced by the mustard seed, make it a slaw to remember.

SERVES 4

Dressing
1/2 teaspoon dried mustard seeds

5 tablespoons raw tahini

2 teaspoons apple cider vinegar

1 teaspoon sun-dried sea salt

2 tablespoons nutritional yeast

2 seeded, soaked dates (see page 42), drained

1 large red cabbage, shredded

1 large savoy cabbage, shredded

3 carrots, shredded

To prepare the dressing, using a mortar and pestle, crush the mustard seeds into a fine powder. In a blender, combine the mustard seed powder, tahini, vinegar, salt, yeast, and dates. Blend well.

In a large serving bowl, toss together the red and savoy cabbages with the carrots. Drizzle the dressing over the top, toss well, and chill for 1 hour before serving.

Root Slaw

Shredded root vegetables of different colors make for a festive and bright salad. They also hold their color for a long time. Root vegetables are sturdy and can be carved and shaped in various ways to add flair and texture to a dish. Experiment with different styles of shredding and slicing to make this dish look unique. Look for the mirin in Japanese markets.

SERVES 4

¼ jicama, shredded

1 beet, shredded

2 carrots, shredded

4 sunchokes (if available), shredded

½ yakon (if available), shredded

2 tablespoons nama shoyu or Bragg Liquid Aminos

2 tablespoons mirin

2 tablespoons flax oil

Juice of ½ lemon

½ teaspoon cumin seeds, ground

½ teaspoon mustard seeds, ground

½ teaspoon kelp powder

In a large serving bowl, combine the jicama, beet, carrots, sunchokes, and yakon. In a blender, combine the shoyu, mirin, oil, lemon juice, cumin, mustard seeds, and kelp powder. Blend until smooth. Pour the shoyu mixture over the roots, toss well, and let sit for 1 hour, mixing once every 15 minutes or so. Serve.

Tabouli

I was introduced to this traditional Middle Eastern vegetarian dish by the little gyro shops of the Lower East Side in New York City. Traditionally, tabouli is made from bulgur or crushed wheat. Sprouted quinoa has almost the same taste and a very similar consistency. I originally made this with ground sprouted wheat but the whole sprouted quinoa has more life force (being whole) and is softer. The quinoa only needs to soak overnight and sit out and sprout for part of a day, and then it's ready for use. Black quinoa can be used for this dish for an exotic look.

Serves 4

3 cups sprouted quinoa (see page 44)

¼ cup olive or flax oil

1 teaspoon sun-dried sea salt

2 tomatoes, finely diced

½ large red onion, minced and rinsed

1 green onion, thinly sliced

1 red bell pepper, seeded and finely diced

½ yellow bell pepper, seeded and finely diced

2 to 3 sprigs of mint, coarsely chopped

¼ cup minced parsley

¼ cup minced cilantro

Juice of 2 lemons

Mixed salad greens, for lining platter

In a bowl, mix the quinoa, oil, and sea salt. Stir well. Add in the tomatoes, onions, green onion, and bell peppers. Mix in the mint, parsley, cilantro, and lemon juice. Stir until the colors are mixed evenly throughout the dish. Serve on a bed of mixed salad greens.

Dressings

Waldorf Salad Dressing

This Waldorf-style dressing is a perfect replacement for the traditional mayonnaise dressing. This recipe has as its base a great raw, vegan mayo replacement. The raw mayo is further enhanced with orange juice, dill, and onion, making an easy and delicious dressing for a Waldorf salad.

MAKES 2½ CUPS

Raw Mayonnaise

½ cup raw tahini

¼ cup freshly squeezed lemon juice

2 tablespoons apple cider vinegar

2 seeded, soaked dates (see page 42), drained

2 tablespoons Bragg Liquid Aminos, or 1 teaspoon sun-dried sea salt

¼ cup freshly squeezed orange juice

2 tablespoons dried dill

2 tablespoons minced onion

1 cup filtered water

Combine the mayonnaise ingredients in a blender and blend until smooth. Add the remaining ingredients and blend until combined. The dressing can be covered and refrigerated for up to 2 days.

Creamy Herb Dressing

Avocados are the best thing to use to make a creamy dressing. It is important to choose a rich, fatty avocado, not a fruity, watery one. Sharwil and Haas avocados are both good choices. If you don't know the variety, it's often a challenge to tell what it will be like inside. Since there are over three hundred varieties of avocado, it's best to try every type you can find, and once you find one you like, use the same type in all of the avocado dishes you like.

MAKES 2 CUPS

1 ripe, fatty avocado, peeled and pitted

2 tablespoons chopped fresh parsley

2 tablespoons chopped fresh cilantro

2 tablespoons chopped fresh basil

Dash of Bragg Liquid Aminos

1 cup filtered water

Combine all of the ingredients in a blender and blend until smooth. The dressing can be covered and refrigerated for up to 1 day.

Spicy Papaya-Lime Dressing

This traditional Hawaiian Island dressing has a fruity flavor with a real kick.

MAKES 3 CUPS

1 ripe, medium to large papaya, peeled

Juice of 1 lime

1 tablespoon cayenne pepper

1 cup filtered water

2 to 3 tablespoons Bragg Liquid Aminos

Seed the papaya, reserving 2 teaspoons of the seeds. In a blender, blend the papaya, lime juice, cayenne, water, and reserved papaya seeds until smooth. Add the Braggs to taste. The dressing can be covered and refrigerated for up to 3 days.

Green Goddess Dressing

There are many dressings out there called "Green Goddess." This recipe was the Raw Experience version. I don't know what is in any of the other ones, but I do know that this was created out of my garden. It was composed from the gifts of the earth goddess, and since the dressing was green, I called it Green Goddess.

MAKES 3 CUPS

1 cup sunflower sprouts
   (see page 44)

2 tablespoons chopped fresh
   parsley

2 tablespoons chopped fresh dill

2 tablespoons chopped fresh
   cilantro

Juice of 1 lemon

2 tablespoons Bragg Liquid
   Aminos

1 cup filtered water

Combine all of the ingredients in a blender and blend until smooth. The dressing can be covered and refrigerated for up to 1 day.

Mango-Ginger Vinaigrette

This Asian-style dressing is sweet and tangy.

MAKES 2 CUPS

1 ripe mango, peeled and
   seeded

3-inch piece fresh ginger, peeled

3 tablespoons apple cider
   vinegar

1 cup filtered water

Juice of 1 lemon

Place all of the ingredients in a blender and blend well. The dressing be covered and refrigerated for up to 4 days.

Herbed Vinaigrette

Centuries ago, Europeans began scenting their oils or vinegars with herbs by leaving herb sprigs to sit in glass jars of oils and vinegars for months, and even years, in the dark to slowly extract the essence of the plant. This vinaigrette is a tribute to that tradition. If you like, keep the herbs whole and place the ingredients in a covered glass jar, leave it to sit in a cool dark place for a month or so, and then blend.

MAKES ¾ CUP

¼ cup olive oil

¼ cup red wine vinegar or apple cider vinegar

2 tablespoons Bragg Liquid Aminos

1 clove of garlic, crushed

3 sprigs fresh parsley, chopped

4 sprigs fresh dill, chopped

3 sprigs fresh cilantro, chopped

Combine all of the ingredients in a blender or food processor and purée until smooth. The dressing can be covered and refrigerated for up to 4 days.

Carrot-Cashew-Ginger Dressing

This Raw Experience classic is zingy and creamy. Some people even eat it as a soup.

MAKES 2½ CUPS

6 carrots

1-inch piece fresh ginger

2 tablespoons soaked cashews (see page 42), drained

2 tablespoons Bragg Liquid Aminos

Process the carrots through a juicer into a large measuring cup (you should have approximately 2 cups). Reserve ¼ cup of carrot pulp from juicing the carrots. Process the ginger through the juicer into the bowl of a food processor. Add the carrot juice and the cashews and process until smooth. Add the reserved carrot pulp and Braggs and pulse once or twice to combine. The dressing can be covered and refrigerated for up to 2 days.

Sweet Mustard Dressing

Flavors often complement each other. This dressing is spiced by the seed of the mustard plant and tempered by the sweetness of the carrot juice and dates. Using orange juice to replace the dates results in a tangier flavor.

MAKES 1½ CUPS

4 carrots

3 seeded, soaked dates (see page 42), drained, or ½ cup freshly squeezed orange juice

1 teaspoon ground mustard

2 tablespoons Bragg Liquid Aminos, or a pinch of sun-dried sea salt

1 tablespoon nutritional yeast

Process carrots through a juicer into a bowl (you should have about 1⅓ cups). Combine the carrot juice and remaining ingredients in a blender and blend until smooth. The dressing can be covered and refrigerated for up to 2 days.

Peanut-Curry Dressing

From India to Thailand, curry is used in many cuisines. Curry powder is actually a mixture made of many spices from a combination of plants. Turmeric, ginger, ajowan, and other spices are all parts of making curry powder. There is also a tree called curry leaf, which produces a very aromatic and spicy leaf that is a common ingredient in many Indian curry powders.

MAKES 2½ CUPS

1 cup soaked peanuts (see page 42), drained

1 teaspoon curry powder

1 tablespoon Bragg Liquid Aminos

½-inch piece fresh ginger, peeled

1 cup filtered water

Combine all of the ingredients in a blender or food processor and blend or pulse until smooth. The dressing can be covered and refrigerated for up to 2 days.

Avocado-Parsley Dressing

This creamy dressing has both strong and subtle flavors. The parsley gives the dressing an herbal and earthy tone, while the lemon's acidity cuts through the fat of the avocado and offers a light yet smooth texture.

MAKES 2 CUPS

1 ripe avocado, peeled and pitted

1/2 cup loosely packed parsley leaves

1 tablespoon Bragg Liquid Aminos

1 teaspoon ground cumin

Juice of 1/2 lemon

1 cup filtered water

Combine all of the ingredients in a blender or food processor and blend or pulse until smooth. The dressing can be covered and refrigerated for up to 1 day.

Miso-Tahini Dressing

This Asian-style dressing was by far the most popular choice for salads at the Raw Experience. It is salty and creamy and seems to bathe the salad in a divine nectar. Well-aged (two years or longer) white miso is what gives the flavor to this dressing, and the tahini is what makes it creamy.

MAKES 1 1/2 CUPS

2 tablespoons raw tahini

2 heaping tablespoons white miso

1 seeded, soaked date (see page 42), drained

1 cup filtered water

Juice of 1 lemon

Combine all of the ingredients in a blender and blend until smooth. The dressing can be covered and refrigerated for up to 3 days.

Italian Dressing

The herbs used in this recipe are some of the easiest to grow at home. Fresh basil, oregano, cilantro, and parsley can all add true flavor to your meals. Each also produces a flower that makes a beautiful garnish and helps bring out the subtler flavors.

MAKES 2½ CUPS

2 tablespoons chopped basil

2 tablespoons chopped fresh oregano

2 tablespoons chopped fresh cilantro

2 tablespoons chopped fresh parsley

Juice of 1 lemon

4 teaspoons apple cider vinegar

1 tablespoon olive oil

1 tablespoon Bragg Liquid Aminos

½ cucumber, thickly sliced

1 tablespoon dried onion flakes

1 teaspoon paprika

1 cup filtered water

Combine all of the ingredients in a blender or food processor and blend or pulse until smooth. The dressing can be covered and refrigerated for up to 2 days.

Cucumber-Dill Dressing

This is a nice light dressing that is perfect when you want the flavor of the salad to be stronger than that of the dressing. Its flavor is sweet and sour yet not overpowering.

MAKES 2 CUPS

1 cucumber, thickly sliced

¼ cup chopped fresh dill

1 tablespoon Bragg Liquid Aminos

Juice of ¼ lemon

1 cup filtered water or cucumber juice (from about 2 cucumbers)

Combine all of the ingredients in a blender and blend until smooth. The dressing can be covered and refrigerated for up to 2 days.

Almond-Cumin Dressing

This simple dressing has a rich and robust flavor. Cumin seed is the dominant flavor, giving it an earthy taste.

MAKES 1½ CUPS

½ cup sprouted almonds (see page 44)

1 cup filtered water

2 teaspoons Bragg Liquid Aminos

1 teaspoon ground cumin

Combine all of the ingredients in a blender or food processor and blend or pulse until smooth. The dressing can be covered and refrigerated for up to 2 days.

Savory Soups

Creamy Carrot-Ginger Soup

This smooth and spicy soup was one of the most popular soups at The Raw Experience.

SERVES 4

½-inch piece fresh ginger

6 large carrots

1 ripe avocado, peeled and pitted

2 tablespoons loosely packed cilantro leaves

1 tablespoon Bragg Liquid Aminos

1½ cups White Sauce (page 129)

Black sesame seeds, for garnish

Finely grate the ginger on a ginger grater or fine grater to extract its juice (you should have about 1 teaspoon). Using a homogenizing juicer, homogenize the carrots (you should have about 2 cups).

In a blender, blend the ginger and carrot juices, avocado, 2 tablespoons of the cilantro, and the Braggs until smooth. Pour the soup into individual serving bowls, top each with about ⅓ cup of the sauce, and garnish with the sesame seeds.

Tom Yum

This traditional Thai-style soup is my personal favorite. I love coconuts and this soup is all about the coco. I like to use different ages of coconut meat to get varied textures. A more mature nut makes a chunky soup, while a younger one makes a creamy soup. I also like to use a variety of hot peppers: jalapeño, serrano, and even the super-spicy Thai chile, just to get a wide range of spiciness. Some peppers are hot as you eat them, others after you eat them; my favorite are hot only when you stop eating them.

SERVES 2 TO 4

1 coconut

7 leaves basil, plus additional for garnish

3 leaves oregano

5 sprigs cilantro, stemmed

½ Thai, jalapeño, or serrano chile, seeded and minced

2 tablespoons Bragg Liquid Aminos or nama shoyu

Open the coconut with a machete, cleaver, drill, or knife. Pour the coconut water into a blender. With a metal spoon scoop out the coconut meat and place in the blender with the coconut water. Add the 7 leaves of basil, the oregano, cilantro, chile, and Braggs, and blend until smooth. Pour the soup into individual serving bowls, and garnish each with a few basil leaves.

Maui Onion Gazpacho

The Maui onion is a special thing. It grows up at high elevations on the side of Haleakala crater. The onion is crisp and sweet, almost like an apple. In fact, there are people on Maui who eat them whole. Maui onions are what make this soup so good. If you don't have access to them, then find a suitable sweet onion to replace it with.

SERVES 2 TO 4

3 large tomatoes

1 Maui onion, diced (about ¾ cup) and rinsed

1 yellow or red bell pepper, seeded and coarsely chopped

1 clove garlic

1 ripe tomato, chopped

1 cucumber, peeled and chopped

2 tablespoons chopped fresh dill

Juice of 1 lemon

1 to 2 cups filtered water

Bragg Liquid Aminos or sun-dried sea salt

Using a homogenizing juicer, homogenize the tomatoes (you should have about 2 cups). Place the onion, pepper, and garlic in a food processor. Pulse a few times to blend slightly. Add the chopped tomato, cucumber, dill, lemon juice, tomato juice, and 1 cup of the water. Pulse a few more times, until thin but still chunky. If the soup is too thick, add up to 1 cup of the remaining water, and pulse just once or twice to combine. Do not blend until smooth. Add the Braggs to taste. Serve immediately.

Gazpacho

Many people think of soups as something warm or hot. Yet in the heat of the summer, most people don't want a hot soup. Gazpacho is a delicious raw soup traditionally served chilled. The soup originated in the Andalusia region of southern Spain, and is the basis for this amazing creation.

SERVES 2 TO 4

2 large or 3 medium tomatoes

2 cups diced tomatoes (approximately 4 tomatoes)

1 small onion, minced and rinsed

1 cucumber, diced

2 green onions, chopped

Juice of 1 orange

Juice of 1 large lemon

1 clove garlic, crushed

2 tablespoons apple cider vinegar

2 tablespoons olive or flax oil (optional)

⅓ cup coarsely chopped fresh parsley

1 teaspoon coarsely chopped fresh tarragon

1 teaspoon ground cumin

⅓ cup coarsely chopped fresh basil

⅓ cup coarsely chopped fresh cilantro

Pinch of ground cayenne pepper (optional)

Bragg Liquid Aminos or sun-dried sea salt

Juice the tomatoes using a juicer or purée them in a blender and strain. Set aside.

In a food processor, pulse the diced tomatoes, onion, cucumber, and green onions only a few times to mix and chop the ingredients, not to grind them. In a blender, combine the reserved tomato juice, orange juice, lemon juice, garlic, vinegar, and oil. Add the parsley, tarragon, cumin, basil, cilantro, and cayenne pepper, and blend well. In a large bowl, combine the chopped vegetables with the blended soup. Add the Braggs to taste. Chill for about 2 hours before serving.

Creamy Red Pepper Soup

This soup has a bright and sweet flavor that is well supported by the richness of the avocado.

SERVES 2 TO 4

1 red bell pepper, seeded and chopped

1 ripe avocado, peeled and pitted

2 cups filtered water

Leaves from 1 sprig oregano

2 tablespoons chopped fresh cilantro

2 tablespoons chopped fresh parsley

Bragg Liquid Aminos

Black sesame seeds, for garnish

Place the bell pepper, avocado, water, oregano, cilantro, and parsley in a blender, and blend until smooth. Add the Braggs to taste. Pour into serving bowls and garnish with the sesame seeds.

Cucumber-Dill Soup

There is a cucumber called the lemon cucumber that is yellow and round instead of green and long. Lemon cucumbers add an extra flavor to this soup. If you can get them, use them; if not, regular cucumbers will work.

SERVES 2 TO 4

1 cup sunflower sprouts (see page 44)

2 cups filtered water

1 large cucumber, peeled and chopped

2 tablespoons loosely packed fresh dill leaves, plus additional for garnish

Pinch of nutritional yeast

Bragg Liquid Aminos

In a blender, blend the sunflower sprouts and water until smooth. Add the cucumber, the 2 tablespoons dill, and the yeast, and blend until smooth. Add the Braggs to taste. Pour into bowls and serve, garnished with the additional dill leaves.

Corn Chowder

On a visit to Georgia, a friend of mine turned me on to raw corn chowder. It was summer and corn was readily available, so each night we experimented with new evolutions of corn chowder. We decided this final version was the perfect chowder.

SERVES 2 TO 4

½ cup sprouted almonds
   (see page 44)

1 cup filtered water

1 clove garlic

¼ cup coarsely chopped fresh
   cilantro

2 large carrots, shredded

1 cup fresh corn kernels
   (approximately 2 ears corn)

2 tablespoons chopped onion,
   rinsed

Pinch of nutritional yeast

Bragg Liquid Aminos, for
   seasoning

Place the almond sprouts, water, garlic, and cilantro in a blender, and blend until creamy. Add the carrots, corn, onions, and yeast and blend until chunky. Add the Braggs to taste. Pour into bowls and serve.

Borscht

This classic cabbage and beet soup is known throughout Russia and the Slavic region of Europe. Borscht is hearty, healthy, and fun to say.

SERVES 2 TO 4

2 to 3 cups chopped red
   cabbage

1 beet, shredded

2 tablespoons red miso

1 clove garlic

1 cup filtered water

In a blender, blend the cabbage, beet, miso, garlic, and water until smooth. Pour into bowls and serve.

Creamy Carrot Ginger Soup
(page 110)

Nori Rolls
(page 167)

Pesto Pizza
& Traditional Pizza

(page 161)

Thai Curry

(page 165)

Angel Hair with Marinara

(page 164)

Tribal Wild Rice Salad

(page 155)

Papaya Fundae

(page 52)

Carob-Hazelnut Torte

(page 173)

Cascadilla Soup

Cascadilla means "cascade" or "waterfall" in Spanish, which is an accurate description of the outpouring of flavor from this sweet and tangy soup.

SERVES 2 TO 4

5 tomatoes

1 avocado, peeled and pitted

1 red bell pepper, seeded and chopped

1 cucumber, chopped

1 green onion, chopped

1 clove garlic, crushed

2 seeded, soaked dates (see page 42), drained

1 teaspoon chopped fresh dill

Bragg Liquid Aminos, for seasoning

Using a homogenizing juicer, homogenize the tomatoes (you should have about 4 cups of juice). In a blender, blend the tomato juice and avocado. Add the bell pepper, cucumber, green onion, garlic, dates, and dill, and blend well. Add the Braggs to taste. Pour into bowls and serve.

Pea Soup

Fresh peas are a fun summertime treat. Peas still in the pod are always the sweetest—plus they're fun to shuck.

SERVES 2 TO 4

2 cups shelled fresh peas (approximately 2 pounds peas in their pods)

½ avocado, peeled and pitted

¼ cup loosely packed fresh cilantro leaves, plus additional for garnish

1 cup filtered water

Bragg Liquid Aminos, for seasoning

Place the peas, avocado, the ¼ cup cilantro, and water in a blender and blend until smooth. Add the Braggs to taste. Serve in bowls, garnished with the additional cilantro.

Cream of Zucchini Soup

Creamy soups of any kind require some kind of fat to make them creamy. Avocado, soaked nuts, or coconut are the traditional raw sources. This recipe uses cashews, which, of all the nuts, provides the creamiest consistency.

SERVES 2 TO 4

¼ cup soaked cashews (see page 42), drained

½ cup sprouted almonds (see page 44)

2 large zucchini, chopped

2 tablespoons chopped fresh cilantro

2 tablespoons chopped fresh parsley

2 cups filtered water

Bragg Liquid Aminos, for seasoning

Dulse flakes, for garnish

In a blender, blend the cashews and almond sprouts until smooth. Add the zucchini, cilantro, parsley, and water, and blend until smooth. Add the Braggs to taste. Serve in bowls, garnished with the dulse flakes.

Rosy Sea Soup

Dulse is a purple North Atlantic sea vegetable that has a smooth and silky texture and is not overly salty. Dulse doesn't need to be soaked before use because it is so soft to begin with. Dulse is sold dried, whole, or as flakes.

SERVES 2 TO 4

1 beet

2 cups Almond Mylk (page 55)

½ cup dulse flakes

1 avocado, peeled and pitted

Bragg Liquid Aminos, for seasoning

Using a homogenizing juicer, homogenize the beet into a measuring cup (you should have about ¼ cup). In a blender, blend the mylk, dulse, beet juice, and avocado until smooth. Add the Braggs to taste. Pour into bowls and serve.

Almond-Onion-Parsley Soup

An almond can only sprout slightly at room temperature. For almonds to be able to fully sprout and grow into a tree they require a temperature of 57°F. Soaked and germinated almonds still have a higher nutritional value than the original nut and are far tastier than a fully sprouted almond.

SERVES 2 TO 4

1 tablespoon cumin seeds

½ cup sprouted almonds (see page 44)

2 cups filtered water

½ cup loosely packed fresh parsley leaves

1 teaspoon chopped fresh oregano

1 clove garlic, crushed

1 tablespoon olive oil

Bragg Liquid Aminos, for seasoning

⅓ cup minced sweet onion

¼ cup chopped fresh parsley, for garnish

Using a coffee grinder or small food processor, grind the cumin seeds into a powder. In a blender, blend the almonds and water until smooth. Add the ½ cup parsley leaves, the oregano, ground cumin, garlic, and oil and blend until smooth. Add the Braggs to taste. Pour the soup into individual bowls, stir in the onion, and garnish with the chopped parsley.

Pesto Soup

This Raw Experience creation has a robust flavor and chunky texture that make it "soupreme!"

SERVES 2 TO 4

10 large fresh basil leaves

1 clove garlic

¼ cup pine nuts

1 tablespoon red miso

1 tablespoon nutritional yeast

2 cups filtered water

2 cups diced tomato (about 4 tomatoes)

¼ cup diced red bell pepper

2 tablespoons shredded carrots

2 tablespoons shredded beets

2 tablespoons minced onion, rinsed

1 tablespoon Bragg Liquid Aminos

Basil flowers, for garnish

Place the basil, garlic, pine nuts, miso, and yeast in a blender and blend while gradually adding the water. Add the tomatoes, bell pepper, carrots, beets, onion, and Braggs, and pulse until chunky. Serve in bowls, garnished with the basil flowers.

Spirulina-Avocado Soup

Spirulina offers a wealth of nutrition providing an abundance of vitamins and minerals. This smooth and silky soup is power packed and great tasting.

SERVES 2 TO 4

1 large ripe avocado, peeled and pitted

1 cup filtered water

2 tablespoons chopped fresh cilantro, plus additional for garnish

2 tablespoons Bragg Liquid Aminos

2 teaspoons powdered spirulina

Juice of 1/2 lemon

In a blender, blend the avocado, water, 2 tablespoons cilantro, Braggs, spirulina, and lemon juice until smooth. Serve in bowls, garnished with the additional cilantro.

Cauliflower Chowder

This creamy soup is a welcome addition to any raw cook's repertoire. The flavor of cauliflower and almonds creates a synergistic combination that tastes something like cooked rice. This chowder is flavorful and fun.

SERVES 2 TO 4

2 tablespoons shredded carrot

1 cup sprouted almonds (see page 44)

2 cups filtered water

2 tablespoons chopped onions

1 head cauliflower, chopped (about 2 cups)

2 tablespoons nutritional yeast

Bragg Liquid Aminos

Place the almonds, carrots, and water in a blender, and blend until smooth. Add the onions, cauliflower, and yeast, and blend until creamy. Add the Braggs to taste. Pour into bowls and serve.

Cream of Broccoli Soup

Broccoli and cauliflower are two of the most beautiful plants in nature. When flowering, these members of the Brassica *genus have giant bulbous flower heads surrounded by olive green, cabbagelike leaves. Broccoli stems can be used as well as the flowering part—just peel and use.*

SERVES 2 TO 4

- 1 cup sprouted almonds (see page 44)
- 3 cups filtered water
- 1 small head broccoli, chopped (about 2 cups)
- ½ cup chopped red onion
- ¼ cup loosely packed fresh parsley leaves
- 2 tablespoons nutritional yeast
- 1 tablespoon Bragg Liquid Aminos
- 2 tablespoons minced onion, for garnish
- 2 tablespoons chopped cilantro, for garnish

In a blender, blend the almonds and the water until smooth. Stir in the broccoli, red onion, parsley, yeast, and Braggs. Spoon the soup into individual serving bowls. Top each with a little of the minced onion and cilantro and serve.

Curried Almond Soup

Many Indian restaurants in New York City use almonds in their cooking, and that was the original inspiration for this unique and delightful soup.

SERVES 2 TO 4

6 carrots

2 cups sprouted almonds
  (see page 44)

1 cup filtered water

1 teaspoon turmeric

1 teaspoon Bragg Liquid
  Aminos

1 teaspoon ground cumin

1 teaspoon curry powder, or
  1 curry leaf

1 teaspoon nutritional yeast

Shredded carrot, for garnish

Using a homogenizing juicer, homogenize the carrots (you should have about 2 cups). In a blender, grind together the almonds and carrot juice until smooth. Add the water, turmeric, Braggs, cumin, curry powder, and yeast, and blend well. Serve in bowls, garnished with the shredded carrots.

Sweet Potato Soup

To make sweet potatoes more palatable, soak them in water with a bit of sea salt for at least 2 hours. This will help pull out some of the starchy taste and soften the potato for blending.

SERVES 2 TO 4

3 carrots

2 sweet potatoes, peeled and
  shredded (about 2 cups)

2 seeded, soaked dates
  (see page 42), drained

¼ teaspoon ground cardamom

1 cup filtered water

Bragg Liquid Aminos, for
  seasoning

Using a homogenizing juicer, homogenize the carrots (you should have about 1 cup). Place the sweet potato in a bowl, cover with water, and soak for at least 2 hours. Drain. In a blender, blend the sweet potato and the carrot juice. Add the dates, cardamom, and water, and blend until creamy. Add the Braggs to taste.

Appetizers

Pesto Wraps

These delightful little treats were one of the many bite-sized creations that I came up with for a catering gig, and they became such a hit that people requested them forever after.

SERVES 4 TO 6

3 large zucchini, peeled
Pinch of sun-dried sea salt
Juice of ½ lemon

Presto Pesto
2 cups walnuts
2 cups loosely packed fresh
    green and purple basil leaves
3 cloves garlic
1 heaping tablespoon red miso

2 tomatoes, cubed
Chopped green and purple
    basil, for garnish

Using a vegetable peeler or mandoline, cut thin, wide strips lengthwise down the zucchini. Place the zucchini strips in a bowl, cover with water, add the sea salt and lemon juice, and soak for 2 hours, or until they taste clean (not starchy). Drain, rinse, and drain again.

To prepare the pesto, place the walnuts, basil leaves, and garlic in a homogenizing juicer or food processor, and homogenize, creating an oily paste. Transfer the paste to a bowl and stir in the red miso.

To prepare each wrap, lay a zucchini strip flat on the workspace. Drop a teaspoon of pesto in the center of the zucchini strip. Press a small piece of tomato into the pesto. Fold or roll up the zucchini strip. Secure the wrap with a toothpick or place it seam side down on a serving plate. Serve garnished with the chopped green and purple basil.

Flax-Dulse Chips

Flax crackers are possibly the simplest chip or cracker to make and are a crunchy delight. All you will want is "just the flax, ma'am."

SERVES 2 TO 4

3 cups flax seeds
4 cups filtered water
¼ cup dulse flakes

Place the flax seeds in a bowl, cover with the water, and soak for 15 minutes. Mix in the dulse flakes. Drain through a sieve. Using one of the methods described on page 45, thinly spread the flax-seed mixture ¼ inch thick on the appropriate drying surface for the chosen method. Dry for 18 hours, or until crispy.

Cabbage Rolls

Cabbage provides some of the more durable leaves in the vegetable kingdom. Cabbage leaves can be used as a salad bowl, as a burrito "tortilla," or, in this case, as the wrap for cabbage rolls. This Asian-style dish was modeled after a Chinese cabbage roll that I used to eat after kung fu class.

SERVES 4

- 8 sturdy cabbage leaves
- ½ cup sprouted mung beans (see page 44)
- 1 cup shredded red cabbage
- 1 cup shredded napa cabbage
- ½ cup shredded carrots
- ¼ cup sea palm (wet)
- 2 tablespoons white sesame seeds
- 2 tablespoons black sesame seeds
- Juice of 1 large lemon
- 1 teaspoon mirin or rice wine vinegar
- 1 teaspoon sesame oil
- 1 teaspoon Bragg Liquid Aminos or nama shoyu
- 1 teaspoon raw tahini or pumpkin-seed butter

Place the cabbage leaves on a plate in the refrigerator (this will help soften them up for rolling). In a large bowl, combine the mung sprouts, shredded cabbages, and carrots. Mix well. Add the sea palm and sesame seeds and mix well. In a blender, combine the lemon juice, mirin, sesame oil, Braggs, and tahini. Blend well. Pour the lemon juice mixture into the bowl containing the shredded cabbage, and toss to combine. Cover and refrigerate for 2 hours before assembling the rolls.

To prepare each roll, fill a whole cabbage leaf with ½ cup of the shredded cabbage mixture. Fold the ends in tightly to enclose the filling, then finish by rolling up the leaf in the opposite direction (like a burrito). Repeat for the remaining rolls and serve.

Tofu-Stuffed Cherry Tomatoes

Tofu is traditionally a live-cultured food composed mostly of a living bacteria known as Aspergillis oryzae. Most companies pasteurize (cook) their tofu so it doesn't ferment too far, and in doing so, kill all of its living cultures. A true unpasteurized tofu is a living food but not a raw food because it is grown on cooked soy beans. The tofu recipe below is for a sprouted tofu that is both raw and live. Tofu takes time to master, so be patient and your tofu will be well cultured.

SERVES 4 TO 6

Basic Tofu

1 cup slightly sprouted soybeans (tail should just be poking out of the bean; see page 44)

2 to 4 tablespoons filtered water

1 teaspoon nigari

1 teaspoon miso

¼ cup diced yellow bell pepper

¼ cup chopped onion, minced and rinsed

1 clove garlic, pressed

2 tablespoons finely chopped fresh parsley

2 tablespoons finely chopped fresh cilantro

Juice of ½ lemon

Bragg Liquid Aminos, for seasoning

20 cherry tomatoes

2 teaspoons paprika, for garnish

To prepare the tofu, rinse the sprouted soy beans well. Using a food processor, grind the sprouted soy beans with just enough water to create a thick paste. Place the sprouted soy beans in a bowl and stir in the nigari and the miso. Cover the tofu with a piece of cheesecloth. Place a second, smaller bowl inside of the first, pressing so that it presses down on the tofu. (You may need to put a brick or jug of water in the second bowl to add weight.) Leave the tofu in a warm (70 to 85°F), dark place for 24 hours, or until it's dry and firm. Remove the tofu from the bowl and, using the cheesecloth or a silk screen, squeeze out any remaining water.

In a large bowl, mix the tofu, bell pepper, onion, garlic, parsley, and cilantro. Stir well. Add the lemon juice and the Braggs to taste.

Scoop out the cherry tomatoes using a tomato corer or a sharp paring knife. Fill each tomato with a small amount of the tofu mixture and serve, garnished with the paprika.

Corn Chips

Dehydration removes water while leaving the enzymes and nutrition of the dehydrated food intact. Drying corn concentrates its flavor, and drying the coconut makes it crunchy and oily—giving these corn chips great flavor and big crunch.

SERVES 4

2 cups fresh corn kernels (approximately 4 ears corn)

1 cup young coconut meat

¼ cup dried cilantro

Squirt of freshly squeezed lime juice

Pinch of sun-dried sea salt

In a food processor, process the corn and the coconut meat until well combined. Add in the cilantro, lime juice, and sea salt and continue to pulse a few times until chunky. Spread in a single sheet about ¼ inch thick on a dehydrator sheet or on a flat piece of ceramic. Using one of the methods described on page 46, dehydrate the corn chip mixture for 5 hours, or until dry on top. Flip and continue to dry for 5 more hours. Cut into triangles and dry until crisp, about 2 more hours. Keep in a sealed bag or container to maintain crispiness.

Celery and Almond Butter

This was a standard snack in my school lunch and possibly the first recipe I ever learned to make. I never could get enough of them then, and I still can't now.

SERVES 2 TO 4

1 bunch celery, separated into stalks and trimmed

1 cup sprouted almonds (see page 44 or raw almond butter

½ cup soaked raisins (see page 42), drained

Break the celery stalks in half and peel off the major strings. Cut the celery into uniform 5-inch pieces. In a food processor, blend the almonds and raisins. Spread the almond mixture on the celery sticks and serve.

Veggie Kabobs

This dish has a high entertainment value. There is something to be said for fun food. These display beautifully and are almost as enjoyable to make as they are to eat.

SERVES 4

Marinade

2 teaspoons olive oil

¼ cup Bragg Liquid Aminos

2 cups filtered water

2 tablespoons apple cider vinegar

1 clove garlic, pressed

Juice of ½ lemon

Pinch of paprika

Pinch of chile powder

Pinch of dried cilantro

10 cherry tomatoes

1 avocado, peeled, pitted, and cubed

1 onion, cubed and separated into thin squares

10 pitted olives

1 large red bell pepper, seeded and cut into chunks

1 small pineapple, peeled and cut into chunks

To prepare the marinade, in a large bowl, combine the olive oil, Braggs, water, vinegar, garlic, lemon juice, paprika, chile powder, and cilantro. Mix well.

To prepare the kabobs, spear the tomatoes, avocado, onion, olives, bell pepper, and pineapple onto 10-inch wooden skewers, alternating ingredients so that the tastes and colors mix.

Place the kabobs in a shallow bowl and pour the marinade over them. Marinate the kabobs for at least 1 hour and up to 10 hours before serving.

Mini Pizzas

This may be one of the ultimate recipes in the world of raw-food cuisine. This mini-pizza recipe will convince anyone that raw food isn't just salads and nuts.

SERVES 4

Dough for 4 mini pizzas
(recipe follows)

2 cups Red Sauce (page 129)

2 cups White Sauce (page 129)

½ cup chopped fresh basil, for
garnish

Beginning 1 day in advance, prepare the pizza crust.

To serve, place the pizza crusts on a tray. Spread ¼ cup of the red sauce on top of each crust, then ¼ cup of the white sauce. Garnish with the basil and serve.

Pizza Crust

MAKES DOUGH FOR 4 MINI PIZZAS

2 cups sprouted buckwheat
or soft wheat, sprouted for
2 days

3 large carrots

2 tablespoons shredded carrot

2 tablespoons shredded beet

2 tablespoons minced onion

¼ cup flax seeds

2 tablespoons finely chopped
fresh parsley

2 tablespoons finely chopped
fresh cilantro

2 tablespoons finely chopped
fresh basil

2 tablespoons nutritional yeast

2 tablespoons caraway seeds

2 tablespoons sun-dried sea salt

Homogenize the sprouted buckwheat with the whole carrots in a homogenizing juicer. In a bowl, mix the wheat mixture with the shredded carrots, beet, and onion. In a coffee grinder or small food processor, grind the flax seeds into a powder. Add the ground flax seeds, parsley, cilantro, and basil to the wheat-carrot mixture. Stir in the yeast and caraway seeds, and add salt to taste. Mix well (you may need to sink your hands into this one).

Using wet hands, press the dough into 3-inch discs, ¼ to ½ inch thick. Using one of the methods described on page 45, dehydrate the crusts for about 12 hours, or until dry. To decrease the drying time, occasionally flip the crusts.

Red Sauce

MAKES 3½ CUPS

7 dry-packed sun-dried tomatoes, soaked in water until soft, and drained

2 large tomatoes, chopped

1 clove garlic

4 fresh basil leaves, chopped

2 tablespoons Bragg Liquid Aminos

2 tablespoons olive oil

1 tablespoon nutritional yeast

Place the sun-dried tomatoes in a blender. Add the chopped tomatoes, garlic, basil, Braggs, olive oil, and yeast. Blend well, until smooth. The sauce should be very thick.

White Sauce

MAKES 3 CUPS

½ cup macadamia nuts

¼ cup pine nuts

½ cup cashews

2 tablespoons olive oil

1 tablespoon Bragg Liquid Aminos

2 teaspoons nutritional yeast

Juice of 1 lemon

1 cup filtered water, plus additional for thinning, if needed

Place the macadamia nuts, pine nuts, and cashews in a bowl, cover with water, and soak for 2 to 6 hours. Drain. Place all of the ingredients in a blender and blend until smooth, adding additional water, if needed, to obtain a creamy consistency.

Potato Chips

This is the raw food solution to the potato chip. These easy-to-make chips are a crispy snack that tastes great with guacamole or salsa.

SERVES 2 TO 4

3 purple potatoes, sliced crosswise ⅛ inch thick

2 tablespoons Bragg Liquid Aminos

2 tablespoons chile powder

1 teaspoon red miso

Filtered water, for soaking

Place the potatoes in a bowl and add the Braggs, chile powder, red miso, and enough water to cover the potato slices. Mix well, then drain. Using one of the methods described on page 45, dehydrate the potato slices on the appropriate surface for the chosen method for 21 hours, or until crispy.

Carrot–Pine Nut Dip

Dips and spreads are a great way to start a meal. This creamy carrot dip keeps them coming back for more, so make a lot.

SERVES 2 TO 4

4 carrots

2 cups pine nuts, soaked for 2 hours and drained

¼ cup loosely packed parsley

2 tablespoons loosely packed cilantro leaves

3 tablespoons Bragg Liquid Aminos or nama shoyu

2 loaves Carrot-Almond Essence Bread (page 150), sliced, for serving

Process the carrots through a juicer into a large measuring cup (you should have about 1 cup). Place all of the ingredients in a blender, and blend until smooth. Pour into a bowl and serve alongside the Carrot-Almond Essence Bread.

Sides

Kim Chee

Kim chee is an Asian version of sauerkraut, or fermented cabbage. Much like durian, the malodorous Malaysian fruit, you just have to get past the smell and you will really enjoy yourself. Kim chee has a tangy and spicy flavor that will keep you coming back for more. It is also considered a healing food because it helps bring healthy balance back to the intestinal flora. To start the culture, you'll need a tablespoon of prepared kim chee. Using some of a previous batch is best, but you can also purchase kim chee—just make sure it's "live" (unpasteurized) kim chee and doesn't contain any sugar or chemicals.

SERVES 4

½ head red cabbage

½ head napa cabbage

1-inch piece fresh ginger

1 heaping tablespoon red miso

1 jalapeño chile, seeded and diced

1 tablespoon prepared kim chee

There are three different traditional styles of chopping the cabbage for this dish: (1) Thai style: shred the cabbage either using the shredding blade of a food processor or a hand shredder; (2) Korean style: slice the cabbage using the small slicing blade of a food processor or by hand using a sharp knife; (3) Hawaiian style: using a blender, a homogenizing juicer, or food processor, grind the cabbage until it becomes mash. Using one method or some combination of the three, prepare the red cabbage and the napa cabbage. Place both cabbages in a large ceramic bowl or a traditional kim chee or sauerkraut crock, and toss.

In a homogenizing juicer, juice the ginger and ¼ cup, firmly packed, of the prepared cabbage. Place the juiced cabbage and ginger in a bowl, add the miso, jalapeño, and prepared kim chee, and stir well. Add this mixture to the tossed cabbage in the bowl and toss well to combine. Cover with a piece of cheesecloth. Place a second bowl of the same size on top of the first. (This second bowl will act as a weight.) Leave in a warm (75 to 90°F), dark location for 2 days. When your kim chee is ready it will smell strong. It is good to know what kim chee should smell like when fully fermented; buy some in a store and get a good smell.

Traditional Guacamole

Avocados may be the most celebrated fruit in the world of raw foods. This traditional guacamole is a Mexican recipe handed down to me by my friend Josh.

SERVES 4

2 very ripe avocados, peeled and pitted

1 large tomato, diced

¼ onion, diced

½ teaspoon sun-dried sea salt

2 tablespoons chopped fresh cilantro

Juice of ½ lemon

Pinch of nutritional yeast

Pinch of cumin

Lettuce leaves or Flax-Dulse Chips (page 123) and sliced veggies, for dipping

In a large bowl, mash the avocados. Add the remaining ingredients and stir well. Roll in lettuce leaves to make burritos, or serve with flax chips and sliced veggies for dipping.

Star Fruit Guacamole

A giant star fruit tree behind the Maui Raw Experience inspired this delicious guacamole.

SERVES 4

2 avocados, peeled and pitted

2 small star fruits, ribs removed and diced

1 tomatillo, diced

¼ cup diced shallot

1 tablespoon Bragg Liquid Aminos

Juice of 1 lemon

2 tablespoons chopped fresh cilantro

Lettuce leaves or Flax-Dulse Chips (page 123) and sliced veggies, for dipping

In a large bowl, mash the avocados. Add the remaining ingredients and stir well. Roll in lettuce leaves to make burritos, or serve with flax chips and sliced veggies for dipping.

Star Fruit Salsa

One winter while vacationing on Maui, I created this fabulous salsa. I had an abundance of star fruits and was going to a potluck gathering. I had had mango salsa and papaya salsa, both of which are Hawaiian specialties, so I decided to discover star fruit salsa. This sweet and tangy salsa was a huge hit and often appeared on the menu at The Raw Experience.

SERVES 4

5 star fruits, ribs removed and diced

1 cup pitted olives, diced

1 small onion, minced and rinsed

1½-inch piece fresh ginger

2 tablespoons minced fresh cilantro

1 tablespoon apple cider vinegar

1 clove garlic, crushed

2 tablespoons Bragg Liquid Aminos

Juice of 1 lemon

Bottom half of a jalapeño chile, seeded and minced

Flax-Dulse Chips (page 123), for serving

In a large bowl, combine the star fruits, olives, and onion. Finely grate the ginger on a ginger grater or fine grater to extract its juice (you should have about 1 tablespoon). Add the ginger juice, cilantro, vinegar, garlic, Braggs, lemon juice, and jalapeño to the star fruit mixture; mix well. Cover and let sit in the refrigerator or at room temperature for 1 to 4 hours, until the flavors mingle. Serve with flax chips.

Tomatillo Salsa

Tomatillos have a high entertainment value because nature decided to make this fruit come complete with wrapping paper. A tomatillo is like a cross between a berry and a green tomato and has papery husk surrounding its fruit.

SERVES 4

1 pound tomatillos, husked and diced (about 3 cups)

1 cup diced, pitted olives

1/2 cup diced yellow bell pepper

1/4 cup diced tomato

1/2 cup diced onion

2 tablespoons minced fresh cilantro

2 tablespoons Bragg Liquid Aminos

Juice of 1 lime

1 habanero chile, seeded and minced

Sliced veggies (such as sunchokes, carrots, or jicama), for dipping

In a large bowl, mix the tomatillos, olives, bell pepper, tomato, onions, and cilantro. Add the Braggs and lime juice and mix well. Add the habaneros to taste. Cover and let sit in the refrigerator or at room temperature for 1 to 4 hours, until the flavors mingle. Serve with sliced veggies for dipping.

Red Pepper–Chipotle Salsa

The chipotle chile (a dried and smoked jalapeño) has a robust and smoky flavor. Both black and red dried chipotles are sold; the red ones seem to have more flavor, but the black ones are far spicier. These chiles are available pickled and in adobo sauce, but only the dried chipotles are raw.

Serves 4

1 chipotle chile

5 dry-packed sun-dried tomatoes

2 red bell peppers, seeded and diced

1 large tomato, cubed

¼ cup diced onion

2 tablespoons minced fresh cilantro

2 leaves fresh basil

1 tablespoon olive oil

½ teaspoon sun-dried sea salt

Juice of ½ lemon

In a small bowl, soak the chipotle and sun-dried tomatoes in water to cover until soft. Drain. Mince the chipotle and sun-dried tomatoes. Set aside. In a large bowl, mix the bell peppers, fresh tomato, and onion. In a blender cup or blender, mix the cilantro, basil, chipotle, sun-dried tomatoes, and olive oil. Blend until the consistency is that of a chunky paste. Add to the large bowl and mix well. Add the sea salt and lemon juice. Mix well. Cover and refrigerate the salsa for 1 to 4 hours, until the flavors mingle.

Chile Mole

Many ingredients go into making a good mole. In Mexico, chocolate or cacao is traditionally used in the preparation of mole. This mole features a range of vegetables and offers many layers of flavor.

SERVES 4

1 large tomato, diced

½ red bell pepper, seeded and diced

½ purple or yellow bell pepper, seeded and diced

1 medium avocado, peeled, pitted, and cubed

1½ cups corn kernels (approximately 3 ears corn)

¼ cup loosely packed fresh parsley leaves

¼ cup loosely packed fresh cilantro leaves

½ cup dry-packed sun-dried tomatoes, soaked until soft and drained

2 tablespoons Bragg Liquid Aminos

2 cloves garlic, pressed

Juice of ½ lemon

1 teaspoon nutritional yeast

Pinch of cayenne pepper

In a bowl, mix the tomato, bell peppers, avocado, and corn. In a blender, blend the parsley, cilantro, sun-dried tomatoes, Braggs, garlic, lemon juice, and yeast until creamy. Season with the cayenne. Add the blended mixture to the bowl containing diced vegetables. Stir until all of the ingredients are evenly combined and a thick consistency is achieved.

Pea Mole

Sometimes avocados aren't available, yet we crave a good guacamole. This pea mole is a great substitute for these occasions. Fresh peas are less oily than avocados but are just as creamy.

SERVES 4

3 cups shelled fresh peas (approximately 3 pounds peas in their pods)

¼ cup loosely packed fresh cilantro leaves

Juice of 1 lime

Pinch of sun-dried sea salt

Cucumber slices or Corn Chips (page 126), for serving

Place the peas, cilantro, lime juice, and sea salt in a food processor and process until smooth. Serve in a bowl alongside the cucumber slices.

Cashew-Beet Pâté

Beets have a high sugar content and cashews are possibly the sweetest nut. Together they help give this pâté a pleasantly sweet flavor.

SERVES 4

2 cups soaked cashews (see page 42), drained

2 large beets, peeled and cut into chunks

2 large carrots

¼ cup minced fresh parsley

¼ cup minced fresh cilantro

2 stalks celery, diced

½ sweet onion, minced and rinsed

1 tablespoon nutritional yeast

2 tablespoons Bragg Liquid Aminos

Cucumber slides, for serving

Using a homogenizing juicer with the blank plate in place, or in a very strong food processor, grind the cashews, beets, carrots, parsley, and cilantro. Transfer to a bowl and mix in the celery, onion, yeast, and Braggs. Serve with cucumber slices.

Carrot-Almond Pâté

This pâté was the house standard at The Raw Experience. Many of the restaurant's dishes, such as the sampler supreme, nori rolls, and even our "rawich," included this pâté. This is a very versatile recipe; try it stuffed in a hollowed cucumber or alongside Corn Chips (page 126).

SERVES 4

9 large carrots

2 cups almonds, sprouted for 1 day (see page 44)

¼ cup loosely packed fresh parsley leaves

¼ cup loosely packed fresh cilantro leaves

¼ cup minced onion, rinsed

5 tablespoons Bragg Liquid Aminos

2 tablespoons nutritional yeast

1 tablespoon olive oil

Using a homogenizing juicer with the blank plate in place, homogenize the carrots, almonds, parsley, and cilantro into a bowl. Mix in the onion, Braggs, yeast, and olive oil, and serve.

Sunny Red Pepper Pâté

The sunflower spends its days following the sun as it journeys across the heavens. It is fun to notice how sunflowers face east in the morning and west in the evening. This recipe features sprouted sunflower seeds.

SERVES 4

2 cups sunflower sprouts
  (see page 44)

½ cup soaked almonds
  (see page 42), drained

1 large red bell pepper, chopped

1 clove garlic, pressed

2 tablespoons chopped
  fresh dill

2 tablespoons chopped fresh
  cilantro

1 red onion, minced and rinsed

Juice of 1 lemon

2 tablespoons Bragg Liquid
  Aminos

2 tablespoons nutritional yeast

In a homogenizing juicer or food processor, grind the sunflower sprouts, almonds, bell pepper, garlic, and herbs. Transfer to a bowl, stir in the onion, lemon juice, Braggs, and yeast, and serve.

Onion-Walnut Pâté

I first made this pâté out of only foraged, wild foods such as wild onions, parsley, English walnuts, and pine nuts, which all grow in Northern California and parts of the Pacific Northwest. I even served it on dandelion greens and nasturtium leaves.

SERVES 2 TO 4

1 small onion, minced

¼ cup loosely packed fresh parsley leaves

2 cups soaked walnuts (see page 42), drained

2 teaspoons pine nuts, soaked 2 hours in water and drained

1 tablespoon Bragg Liquid Aminos

2 tablespoons nutritional yeast

In a homogenizing juicer, homogenize the onion, parsley, walnuts, and pine nuts into a bowl. Add the Braggs and yeast and mix well. Serve.

Colorful Tofu Salad

Eye appeal is important in any dish you create. Sometimes eye appeal is about symmetry and use of complementary colors. In this dish, the vegetables create a medley of hues in contrast to the white tofu background; it is bright and stunning to look at.

SERVES 4

2 cups Basic Tofu (see page 125)

1 small carrot, shredded

1 small beet, shredded

½ small onion, diced

½ red bell pepper, diced

1 tablespoon Bragg Liquid Aminos

1 teaspoon ground cumin

In a large bowl, combine the sprouted tofu, carrots, beets, onions, and bell pepper. Stir in the Braggs and cumin and serve.

Creamy Avocado-Tofu Salad

There is a saying in the world of raw foods that goes something like this: "If it was good before, add some avocado and it will get even better." This tofu salad is as smooth and creamy as can be.

SERVES 4

1 avocado, peeled and pitted

2 cups sprouted tofu (see Basic Tofu on page 125)

¼ cup minced fresh parsley

¼ cup chopped fresh cilantro

2 tablespoons minced onion, rinsed

3 tablespoons Bragg Liquid Aminos

Juice of 1 lemon

2 teaspoons paprika, plus additional for garnish

Pinch of nutritional yeast (optional)

In a large bowl, mash the avocado. Add the tofu, parsley, cilantro, onion, Braggs, lemon juice, the 2 teaspoons paprika, and the yeast, and mix well. Serve garnished with a sprinkle of paprika.

Basic Seed Cheeze

Cultured foods are one of the four living food groups along with fresh foods, sprouted foods, and dried foods. Seed cheeze, a cultured food, is another great way to gain healthy flora. This basic version, like tofu, is very versatile and can be used in many recipes that call for tofu. Seed cheeze can be made from any seed, although sunflower and pumpkin seeds seem to work the best. Dr. Ann Wigmore, the mother of sprouts and wheatgrass, taught me how to make seed cheeze during my time at her school, Dr. Ann Wigmore's Institute for Living Food Studies. This dish is one of the foundations of the living-food movement.

MAKES 4 CUPS

3 cups sunflower, pumpkin, or sesame seeds

Filtered water

1 tablespoon rejuvelac (see page 71) or whey starter (optional)

Place the sunflower seeds in a ½-gallon glass jar and fill the jar full with water. Cover with cloth, screen, or mesh, and soak overnight. The next morning, drain and rinse the seeds. Place the seeds in a food processor and pulse with 2 cups of fresh water a few times, until chunky. Pour into a clean jar. If desired, add the rejuvelac or whey starter to make the seeds culture faster. Place the jar in a dark, warm place for 10 to 12 hours, or only 6 to 8 hours if rejuvelac was added.

The curds (solid part) and whey (liquid part) should separate. The seed cheeze should smell slightly sour and cultured, like yogurt. Drain off as much whey as you can, reserving it for other uses. Squeeze the curds in a piece of cheesecloth to remove the remaining whey. (If you do this over a bowl you can save this whey, too.) The dry curds are the seed cheeze and are now ready for use. To store or shape the cheeze, pack it into a bowl or container, cover, and refrigerate for up to 2 days.

Festive Seed Cheeze

This colorful version of seed cheeze played a key part in The Raw Experience's Nori Rolls (page 167) and earned many smiles from the residents of Maui.

MAKES 5 CUPS

¼ cup pine nuts

2 cups Basic Seed Cheeze (page 144), prepared using sunflower seeds

1 small carrot, shredded

½ yellow bell pepper, diced

1 small beet, shredded

¼ cup minced onion, rinsed

¼ cup loosely packed fresh parsley leaves, minced

¼ cup loosely packed fresh cilantro leaves, minced

3 tablespoons Bragg Liquid Aminos

Juice of ½ lemon

Pinch of nutritional yeast

Using a blender cup or blender, grind the pine nuts into a fine powder. In a large bowl, combine the ground pine nuts, seed cheeze, carrot, bell pepper, beet, and onion. Add the parsley, cilantro, Braggs, lemon juice, and yeast, and mix well. Serve.

Rich and Creamy Seed Cheeze

This recipe for super-smooth seed cheeze once again features the avocado. Avocado trees can grow almost anywhere, although they'll usually only bear fruit in the tropics. In New York City, my mother has grown an avocado tree for over twenty-five years. It was started as a seed when I was a kid and is still in her apartment today. It is kept inside because avocados don't enjoy the cold. It may never fruit, but it is nice to know it is there.

MAKES 3 CUPS

1 ripe avocado, peeled and pitted

2 cups Basic Seed Cheeze (page 144), prepared using sunflower seeds

¼ cup minced fresh parsley

1 teaspoon nutritional yeast

2 tablespoons Bragg Liquid Aminos

In a large bowl, mash the avocado. Stir in the seed cheeze, parsley, yeast, and Braggs, and serve.

Pumpkin-Cashew Seed Cheeze

This recipe includes pumpkin seed cheeze. Pumpkin seeds are rich and oily and add a heartier flavor to this dish. To make pumpkin seed cheeze just follow the instructions for Basic Seed Cheeze, using pumpkin seeds.

MAKES 3½ CUPS

2 cups Basic Seed Cheeze (page 144), prepared using sunflower seeds

1 cup soaked cashews (see page 42), drained

½ cup Basic Seed Cheeze (page 144), prepared using pumpkin seeds

3 tablespoons Bragg Liquid Aminos

In a food processor, blend all of the ingredients until smooth. Transfer to a large bowl and serve.

Herbed Garlic Seed Cheeze

With its garlic and basil, this cheeze has a Italian flair to it.

SERVES 4

5 dry-packed sun-dried tomatoes

2 cups Basic Seed Cheeze
(page 144), prepared using
equal amounts of sunflower
and sesame seeds

2 tablespoons chopped fresh
basil

2 tablespoons chopped fresh
parsley

2 tablespoons chopped fresh
cilantro

2 cloves garlic, crushed

2 tablespoons Bragg Liquid
Aminos

In a small bowl, soak the tomatoes in water to cover until soft. Drain and mince. In a large bowl, combine the tomatoes, seed cheeze, herbs, garlic, and Braggs. Mix well and serve with a smile.

Unstuffing

For Thanksgiving I love to re-create traditional dishes in untraditional ways. This unstuffing is a celebrated hit at every Thanksgiving dinner I've attended.

SERVES 2 TO 4

1 large loaf or 2 small loaves
Herbed Essence Bread
(page 149), crumbled (about
4 cups)

¼ onion, minced and rinsed

2 stalks celery, minced

2 carrots, shredded

¼ cup sunflower seeds

1 teaspoon caraway seeds

2 tablespoons nutritional yeast

2 to 3 tablespoons Bragg Liquid
Aminos

In a large bowl, mix the bread crumbs, onion, celery, and carrots. In a blender cup or a spice grinder, pulverize the sunflower and caraway seeds. Add the seeds to the bowl containing the bread crumb mixture. Add the yeast and up to 3 tablespoons of the Braggs, to taste, and stir well.

Essence Breads

This bread was originally called "Essene bread." The Essenes were a group of people living thousands of years ago in Palestine. The tradition of making Essene bread is discussed in the Essene Gospels, a translation of the Dead Sea Scrolls. The Essenes would sprout their grains, mash them up, and set them in the sun to dry. This sacred bread-making tradition has been handed down over the ages. I decided to evolve the name into Essence Bread because the loaves hold the essence of life. Sprouted grains have a great amount of potential energy, and drying them in the sun concentrates the essential life force contained within.

Essence Breads are created by sprouting grains such as wheat, rye, oat, and kamut or seeds like buckwheat. These grains and seeds are then dried at a low enough temperature to ensure enzyme protection (108°F). Essence Breads can be used as a live alternative to overly processed baked bread, in rawiches or as pizza crusts. You can dry Essence Breads slightly for a soft, doughy texture, or dry the bread totally for a crispy texture that makes great chips and crackers and increases its storage time.

Grains are at their nutritional peak when the sprouting tail is as long as the grain itself. I recommend processing the sprouted grains through a homogenizing juicer with the juicing plate and adding a small amount of water to keep it lubricated. (Added water is only needed when the grains aren't already moist and even then, just 1 or 2 tablespoons per cup of grains will do the job.) Be sure to put a container where the juice normally comes out to catch excess gluten or water. Too much gluten can be difficult to pass through the body. Removing the glutinous part of the grain makes for easier digestion, especially of wheat, a grain known for its high gluten content. Buckwheat contains no gluten and makes awesome bread. The pulp that comes out of the front of the juicer is the usable part of the grain. If a homogenizing juicer is unavailable, the grain can be ground in a food processor, adding just enough water to form a smooth paste. The dough can be shaped into loaves, sticks, or flat crusts.

Herbed Essence Bread

Breads made with herbs are aromatic and savory. In addition to traditional square-shaped loaves, this bread may be pressed into flat circles or squares, rounded loaves, or even stars or hearts.

MAKES 4 LOAVES

2 cups sprouted grain (see page 44), such as wheat, rye, kamut, quinoa, or barley

2 tablespoons minced fresh parsley

2 tablespoons minced fresh cilantro

2 tablespoons minced fresh basil

¼ cup shredded carrot

2 tablespoons minced onions

1 clove garlic, pressed

2 cups flax seeds

Grind the grain in a homogenizing juicer and place it in a large bowl. Add the parsley, cilantro, basil, carrot, onions, and garlic to the grain. Mix well. In a blender cup or blender, grind the flax seeds into a fine powder. Add the flax powder to the bowl and mix well. Divide the dough into 4 equal portions, and press each into a loaf or another shape. Using one of the methods described on page 45, dehydrate the bread for 8 hours and flip. Dry for 4 to 10 more hours (depending on desired moisture level).

Fruit and Nut Essence Bread

Sweet breads are especially good for almond butter and jelly rawiches or as a simple, delicious snack, on their own.

MAKES 4 LOAVES

4 cups sprouted grain (see page 44), such as kamut or rye

5 seeded, soaked dates (see page 42), drained

¼ cup sprouted almonds (see page 44)

¼ cup soaked raisins, (see page 42), drained

2 tablespoons chopped walnuts

Grind the grain in a homogenizing juicer and place in a large bowl. In a blender cup or blender, pulse the dates and the almonds until chunky. Add the date mixture to the bowl containing the grain. Add the raisins and the walnuts. Mix thoroughly. Divide the mixture into four equal portions, and press each into a loaf or a half-dome shape, 2 to 3 inches at its peak. Using one of the methods described on page 45, dehydrate the bread for 8 hours and flip. Dry for 5 to 10 more hours (depending on desired moisture level).

Carrot-Almond Essence Bread

Carrot bread is very much like a doughy carrot cake. This bread is a great breakfast treat.

MAKES 4 LOAVES

- 4 cups sprouted grain (see page 44), such as rye or wheat
- 5 seeded, soaked dates (see page 42), drained
- 1 cup sprouted almonds (see page 44)
- 2 carrots, shredded (about 2 cups)
- 2 teaspoons soaked caraway seeds (see page 42), drained

Grind the grain in a homogenizing juicer and place in a large bowl. In a blender cup or blender, pulse the dates and the almonds until they form a thick paste. Add the date mixture to the bowl containing the grain. Add the carrots and caraway seeds. Mix thoroughly. Divide into four equal portions and press each into a loaf or another shape. Using one of the methods described on page 45, dehydrate the bread for 8 hours and flip. Dry for 5 to 10 more hours (depending on desired moisture level).

Apple-Cinnamon Essence Bread

This bread is another great breakfast treat. It tastes like apple turnovers.

MAKES 4 LOAVES

- 4 cups sprouted grain (see page 44)
- 7 seeded, soaked dates (see page 42), drained
- 1 cup shredded apples (about 1 to 2 apples)
- 1 cup walnuts, chopped
- 2 teaspoons ground cinnamon

Grind the grain, dates, and apples in a homogenizing juicer and place in a large bowl. Stir in the walnuts and cinnamon. Mix thoroughly. Divide into four equal portions and press each into a loaf or another shape. Dry for 8 hours and flip. Dry for 5 to 10 more hours (depending on desired moisture level).

Caraway-Onion Essence Bread

This is a savory bread that has a nice spicy taste to it.

MAKES 4 LOAVES

2 cups sprouted grain (see page 44), such as buckwheat or rye

1 small onion, diced

1 clove garlic

¼ cup soaked caraway seeds (see page 42), drained

Grind all of the ingredients in a homogenizing juicer and place in a large bowl. Mix thoroughly. Divide into four equal portions and press each into a loaf or other shape. Using one of the methods described on page 45, dehydrate the bread for 8 hours and flip. Dry for 5 to 10 more hours (depending on desired moisture level).

Cranberry Sauce

Tart and tangy, this cranberry sauce is a welcome addition to any feast.

SERVES 4

3 cups fresh cranberries, or 1½ cups dried cranberries, soaked in water until soft and drained

5 seeded, soaked dates (see page 42), drained

1 cup soaked raisins, (see page 42), drained

1 teaspoon ground allspice

¼ cup freshly squeezed orange juice

In a blender, blend all of the ingredients until smooth. Transfer to a bowl, cover, and refrigerate until chilled before serving.

Sprouted Hummus

Garbanzo beans, or chickpeas, sprout quickly and easily. When sprouting garbanzos, make certain not to overfill the jar. Garbanzos expand so rapidly that they can shatter a glass jar. The best flavor comes from using garbanzos that have been sprouted for one day.

SERVES 4

4 cups sprouted garbanzo beans (see page 44)

¼ cup chopped fresh parsley

1 clove garlic

¼ cup raw tahini

¼ cup freshly squeezed lemon juice

Sun-dried sea salt

In a homogenizing juicer with the blank plate in place, homogenize the garbanzo beans, parsley, and garlic into a bowl. In a blender, blend the tahini and lemon juice. Stir the lemon-tahini mixture into the bean mixture. Add sea salt to taste. Serve.

Baba Ghanoush

This Middle Eastern dish is hearty and earthy. The longer you marinate the eggplant, the better it gets. Serve the baba ghanoush with Hummus (page 152), Falafel (page 160), or Tabouli (page 99)

SERVES 4

1 large eggplant, peeled and thinly sliced

Generous pinch of sun-dried sea salt

Juice of 1 lemon

1 clove garlic, crushed

1 teaspoon sprouted cumin seeds (see page 44)

¼ cup raw tahini

1 medium onion, minced and rinsed

¼ cup minced fresh parsley

Bragg Liquid Aminos

Put the eggplant in a large bowl, cover with water, add the sea salt and lemon juice, and soak for 4 to 10 hours. (This will help cure the eggplant and improve its flavor.) Drain. In a homogenizing juicer with the blank plate in place, homogenize the eggplant with the garlic and cumin sprouts into a large bowl. Add the tahini, onion, and parsley and mix well. Mix in the Braggs to taste.

Pumpkin Butter

Pumpkins are a curcubit and, like most of their cousins, have a slightly starchy and bitter taste when eaten raw. Soaking pumpkin can greatly improve its flavor. Serve this spread on Fruit and Nut Essence Bread (page 149) or topped with Nut Crème (page 170) as a dessert.

SERVES 4

1 pumpkin (approximately 3 pounds), such as pie pumpkin or sweet pumpkin

Juice of 1 lemon

1 cup soaked pecans (see page 42), drained

1 cup seeded, soaked dates (see page 42), drained

1 teaspoon ground cinnamon

1 teaspoon ground nutmeg

1 teaspoon pure vanilla extract

Peel and seed the pumpkin, reserving the seeds for another use. Cut the flesh into chunks (you should have about 4 cups). Place the pumpkin flesh in a large bowl, cover with water, add the lemon juice, and soak overnight. Drain and rinse the pumpkin and drain again.

In a homogenizing juicer, homogenize the pumpkin with the pecans and dates and place in a large bowl. Mix in the cinnamon, nutmeg, and vanilla.

Tapenade

Olives and sun-dried tomatoes are two of the richest and most concentrated flavors that raw food offers. Combining the two yields this classic Italian spread.

SERVES 2 TO 4

8 dry-packed sun-dried tomatoes, soaked in water until soft and drained

15 pitted olives

2 tablespoons Bragg Liquid Aminos

1 clove garlic

3 sprigs basil

Herbed Essence Bread (page 149) or zucchini slices, for serving

Grind all of the ingredients in a food processor until smooth. Transfer to a bowl. Serve spread on Herbed Essence Bread or zucchini slices.

Entrees

Tribal Wild Rice Salad

Wild rice grows as a seed along the banks of the Great Lakes. Native Americans known as the Chippewa still hand-harvest the wild rice in the traditional manner of their tribe: one person steers the canoe while the other pulls the plants into the boat, threshing the rice from its shaft. Wild rice is one of the few seeds that will sprout anaerobically (without oxygen). Soak the wild rice for 3 to 5 days, changing the water twice a day. Look for hulled hemp seeds in health food stores.

SERVES 4 TO 6

Dressing

4 seeded, soaked dates (see page 42), drained

3 to 5 tablespoons Bragg Liquid Aminos or nama shoyu

Juice of 1 lemon

1 teaspoon flax oil

2 cups sprouted wild rice (see page 44)

1 avocado, peeled, pitted, and cubed

1 yellow bell pepper, seeded and diced

1 Maui or other sweet onion, minced and rinsed

1 Roma tomato, diced

1 mango, peeled, pitted, and diced

¼ cup hulled hemp seeds

Black and white sesame seeds, for garnish

Chopped almonds, for garnish

Field greens, for garnish

To prepare the dressing, place the dates, 3 tablespoons of the Braggs, the lemon juice, and flax oil in a blender and process until creamy. Add up to 2 tablespoons of the remaining Braggs to taste.

In a large bowl, combine the sprouted rice, avocado, bell pepper, onion, tomato, mango, and hemp seeds. Add the dressing and toss well.

To prepare each serving, line a 2-cup bowl with plastic wrap and fill with salad, packing the salad firmly as you go until level. Place an individual serving plate over the top of the bowl and invert. Set the bowl aside and slowly peel away the plastic wrap. Repeat for the remaining servings. Top each with a sprinkling of sesame seeds and almonds. Garnish the edges of the plates with the field greens.

Mexican Wild Rice and Tofu

In many places rice is a staple, or primary food source. Wild rice is very adaptable and can be seasoned with a variety of ethnic ingredients. This entree has a decidedly Mexican flair.

SERVES 4

3 cups sprouted wild rice
(see page 44)

2 small tomatoes, diced

2 tablespoons diced onion

2 tablespoons minced fresh
cilantro

1 red bell pepper, seeded
and diced

1 yellow bell pepper, seeded
and diced

1 clove garlic, pressed

¼ cup Bragg Liquid Aminos, or
1 teaspoon sun-dried
sea salt

1 teaspoon chile powder

½ teaspoon ground cayenne
pepper

Juice of ½ lime

2 cups Basic Tofu (page 125)
or Basic Seed Cheeze
(page 144)

In a large bowl, combine the rice, tomatoes, onion, cilantro, bell peppers, and garlic. Add the Braggs, chile powder, cayenne pepper, and lime juice, and toss well. Serve with the tofu or seed cheeze.

Festive Sprouted Wild Rice

Sprouted black long-grain wild rice has a robust taste and smell. The seeds sprout under water that you change twice a day. When the seeds are rinsed, the earthy aroma rises up. Take a deep inhalation as you pour out the water, and enjoy the scent.

SERVES 4 TO 6

5 cups sprouted wild rice (see page 44)

½ onion, minced and rinsed

1 red bell pepper, diced

1 cup corn kernels (approximately 2 ears corn)

5 tablespoons Bragg Liquid Aminos

3 tablespoons paprika

Juice of 1 orange

In a large bowl, combine the rice, onion, bell pepper, and corn. Stir in the Braggs, paprika, and orange juice. Serve.

Tofu Loaf

The sprouted tofu gives this dish a nice light texture while still having a very meaty taste. For a richer version, use seed cheeze (see pages 144 to 147) in place of the tofu.

SERVES 4

2 cups Basic Tofu (page 125)

1 cup carrot pulp (from juicing carrots)

½ onion, chopped

½ stalk celery, chopped

2 cloves garlic, minced

¼ cup minced fresh parsley

¼ cup raw tahini

2 tablespoons Bragg Liquid Aminos

1 tablespoon nutritional yeast

In a large bowl, combine all of the ingredients. Mix thoroughly. Line a loaf pan with a piece of plastic wrap and press the tofu mixture firmly into the pan. Invert the loaf pan onto a plate. Gently remove the loaf pan and set aside, then carefully peel away the plastic wrap. You may also use your hands to form the tofu mixture into a loaf shape. Serve.

Sunflower-Carrot Croquettes

I first created this delightful little dish for a raw-food housewarming party that I was having. I served the croquettes shaped into stars and hearts, and people loved them.

SERVES 4

6 carrots, chopped

3 cups soaked sunflower seeds (see page 42), drained

1 cup chopped fresh cilantro

¼ cup diced onions

3 tablespoons Bragg Liquid Aminos

2 tablespoons nutritional yeast

Fresh herbs (such as parsley or dill), for garnish

In a homogenizing juicer, homogenize the carrots and the sunflower seeds into a large bowl. Mix in the cilantro, onions, Braggs, and yeast and form into shapes such as circles, stars, or hearts. Arrange on a serving platter and garnish with fresh herbs.

Almond-Corn Croquettes

This evolution of croquettes was a version The Raw Experience served during a Living Thanksgiving celebration on Maui.

SERVES 4

1 cup sunflower seeds

1 cup flax seeds

2 cups sprouted almonds (see page 44)

4 cups fresh corn kernels (approximately 8 ears corn)

¼ cup Bragg Liquid Aminos

¼ cup diced onion

Almond-Cumin Dressing (page 108), for drizzling

2 loaves Caraway-Onion Essence Bread (page 151), for serving

In a coffee grinder or food processor, grind the sunflower seeds and flax seeds into a fine powder. In a homogenizing juicer or a food processor, homogenize or finely grind the seed powders, sprouted almonds, corn, Braggs, and onion and place in a large bowl. Form the mixture into small, 1½-inch loaves. Arrange on a serving plate and drizzle with the salad dressing. Serve, accompanied by the bread.

Tamales

This raw adaptation of the classic Mexican dish is simple to make and tastes delicious.

SERVES 4

1 cup flax seeds

6 cups corn kernels (approximately 12 ears corn)

1 cup dried cilantro

2 teaspoons sun-dried sea salt

3 cups Mexican Wild Rice and Tofu (page 156)

2 cups Red Pepper–Chipotle Salsa (page 137)

2 cups Star Fruit Guacamole (page 134)

In a coffee grinder or food processor, grind the flax seeds into a fine powder. In a food processor, blend the corn, cilantro, salt, and flax powder until well combined but chunky. Pour onto dehydrator sheets or a piece of waxed paper on a flat tray into patties, 1/2 inch thick and 6 inches in diameter, and dry for 8 to 10 hours. Top with 1/2 cup of the rice, 1/4 cup of the salsa, and 1/4 cup of the guacamole. Enjoy!

Middle Eastern Plate

Garbanzo beans play a major role in the cuisine of the Middle East. This Raw Experience classic uses garbanzo beans to make both the falafel-style pizza crust and the hummus spread. The falafel crusts keep quite well and any extra hummus can always be turned into falafel for later use.

SERVES 4

4 falafel crusts (page 160)

2 cups Sprouted Hummus (page 152)

1 tomato, diced

1/4 cup minced onion, rinsed

2 tablespoons diced cucumber

2 tablespoons minced fresh parsley

4 sprig of mint, for garnish

4 olives, for garnish

Place each of the falafel crusts on an individual serving plate. Spread 1/2 cup of the hummus on top of each crust. Sprinkle the tomatoes, onions, cucumber, and parsley evenly over the top of each crust. Garnish with the mint and black olives.

Falafel

This falafel recipe can be prepared as crusts for use in the Middle Eastern Plate, or it can be made into more traditional falafel balls. To make the balls just follow the instructions below and instead of pressing into crusts, roll the mixture into 1-inch balls, then dehydrate for only 8 to 10 hours.

MAKES FOUR 8-INCH CRUSTS OR EIGHT 4-INCH CRUSTS

6 cups sprouted garbanzo
   beans (see page 44)

1 cup loosely packed fresh
   parsley leaves

1 cup raw tahini

1 cup freshly squeezed lemon
   juice

1 onion, minced

2 tablespoons ground cumin

6 tablespoons Bragg Liquid
   Aminos, or 2 tablespoons
   sun-dried sea salt

1 cup sesame seeds

Using a homogenizing juicer with the blank plate in place, homogenize the garbanzo beans and parsley and place in a large bowl. In a blender, blend the tahini, lemon juice, onion, cumin, and Braggs. Stir the tahini mixture into the garbanzo paste. In a spice grinder, grind the sesame seeds into a fine powder. Mix into the garbanzo paste. Press into ¼-inch-thick crusts, 4 or 8 inches in diameter. Using one of the methods described on page 45, dehydrate for 12 to 14 hours, flipping at least once during the drying time.

Pesto Pizza & Traditional Pizza

At The Raw Experience restaurant in San Francisco, we always came up with different pizzas as daily specials, but these two were permanently on the menu.

SERVES 4

4 8-inch Pizza Crusts
  (recipe follows)
1 cup Red Sauce (page 128)
1 cup White Sauce (page 128)
1 cup Pesto (page 123)
1/2 red tomato, diced
1/2 yellow tomato, diced
1 onion, minced and rinsed
1 small beet, shredded
1/2 cup pine nuts, ground
5 purple basil leaves, minced
5 green basil leaves, minced

Place each of the crusts on an individual serving plate. Spread 1/2 cup of the red sauce over each of two of the crusts, followed by 1/2 cup of the white sauce over each. Spread 1/2 cup of the pesto on each of the two remaining crusts. Top all four with the tomatoes, onions, beets, pine nuts, and basil.

Pizza Crusts

MAKES FOUR 8-INCH CRUSTS OR EIGHT 4-INCH CRUSTS

4 cups sprouted wheat
  (see page 44)
1 clove garlic, pressed
1/4 cup minced fresh parsley
1/4 cup minced fresh cilantro
1/4 cup minced fresh basil
1/4 cup sprouted cumin seeds
  (see page 44)
1/4 cup soaked flax seeds
  (see page 42), drained
1 beet, shredded
2 carrots, shredded
1/2 cup minced onion
3 tablespoons Bragg Liquid
  Aminos

Using a homogenizing juicer, homogenize the wheat sprouts with the garlic, parsley, cilantro, basil, cumin seeds, and flax seeds. Place in a large bowl and mix in the beets, carrots, onions, and Braggs. Stir until well mixed, and then press into 1/4-inch thick-crusts, 4 or 8 inches in diameter. Using one of the methods described on page 45, dehydrate the crusts for 12 hours, flipping at least once during drying time.

Lasagna

One of the claims to fame of The Raw Experience was that we could make any cooked-food dish in a raw way. We got a number of requests for a raw lasagna and created this recipe in response. For a while we called it "Living," but eventually we went back to its original name. Versions of this dish are served in raw-food and vegetarian restaurants throughout America.

SERVES 4 TO 8

1 cup filtered water

1 cup freshly squeezed lemon juice

3 tablespoons Bragg Liquid Aminos

1 clove garlic, pressed

1 teaspoon dried parsley

1 teaspoon dried basil

1 eggplant, peeled

2 large zucchini, peeled

1 medium sweet onion, cut into rings

1 cup walnuts

4 cups Red Sauce (page 128)

2 cups White Sauce (page 128)

In a bowl, combine the water, lemon juice, Braggs, garlic, parsley, and basil. Using a vegetable peeler or mandoline with the thinnest blade, slice the eggplant and zucchini lengthwise into long strips. Place the eggplant, zucchini, and onions in a shallow dish and pour the lemon juice mixture over the top. Marinate overnight.

In a blender cup or coffee grinder, grind the walnuts into a fine powder. Moisten the inside of a lasagna dish with water and sprinkle the bottom and sides of the dish with 2 tablespoons of the walnut powder to coat. Cover the bottom of the dish with a layer of the marinated vegetables, and top with 1 cup of the red sauce and 1/2 cup of the white sauce. Repeat three times. Top with the remaining walnut powder. Serve, or dehydrate for 4 hours to concentrate the flavors then serve.

Focaccia

This vegetable-topped bread is a classic Italian meal. It's like pizza without the sauces.

SERVES 4

Garlic-Herb Oil

½ cup olive or flax oil

1 to 2 cloves garlic, pressed

4 leaves fresh basil

1 teaspoon minced fresh
   rosemary

2 cups dry-packed sun-dried
   tomatoes, soaked in water
   until soft, drained, and
   finely chopped

2 red bell peppers, diced

10 pitted olives, sliced crosswise

1 small sweet onion, minced

1 cup pine nuts, finely ground

1 cup loosely packed fresh basil
   leaves, chopped

4 Pizza Crusts (page 161) or
   Herbed Essence Breads
   (page 149)

To prepare the Garlic-Herb Oil, in a bowl combine all of the ingredients. Cover and allow to sit overnight.

In a bowl, combine the sun-dried tomatoes, bell peppers, olives, onion, pine nuts, and basil. Place each of the four crusts on an individual serving plate. Spread ¼ cup to ½ cup of the sun-dried tomato mixture over each crust. Drizzle each focaccia with the Garlic-Herb Oil and serve.

Angel Hair with Marinara

I have always been a strong believer that the key to pasta is in the sauce and not in the pasta. Spaghetti is just flour and water, much like papier-mâché. The noodles are just a carrier. Serve with a green salad and Italian dressing (page 107) and Herbed Essence Bread (page 149) cut into triangles.

SERVES 4

2 large zucchini

1 large yellow summer squash

1 large, fat carrot

1 large red beet

Pinch of sun-dried sea salt

2 cups Red Sauce (page 128)

½ cup pine nuts, finely ground

½ cup pitted olives, sliced

¼ cup loosely packed fresh basil leaves, chopped

5 dry-packed sun-dried tomatoes, soaked in water until soft, drained, and finely chopped

Herbed Essence Bread, cut into triangle-shaped slices, for serving

Use a spiralizer to create spaghetti-like "pasta" or a vegetable peeler to create linguini-style "pasta" of the zucchini, squash, carrot, and beet. Rinse the vegetables well and soak in water with the salt for 1 hour. Drain. In each of four serving bowls, place one quarter of the vegetables. Pour ½ cup of the red sauce over each serving. Top each serving with some of the pine nuts, olives, basil, and sun-dried tomatoes. Serve with the bread.

Thai Curry

Thailand has been heavily influenced by Indian culture. India's religion, music, and especially their food, all have become part of Thailand's heritage. Curries are often thought of as an Indian thing, but Thai versions of curry are just as divine.

SERVES 4

Curry Sauce

1½-inch piece fresh ginger

1 cup soaked peanuts (see page 42), drained

1 cup young coconut meat

½ cup coconut water

1 tablespoon raw almond butter

2 teaspoons Bragg Liquid Aminos

1 clove garlic, pressed

1 teaspoon turmeric

1 teaspoon curry powder

Juice of 1 orange

1 Thai chile

¼ head cauliflower, diced

1 small carrot, shredded

¼ head red cabbage, shredded

½ large cucumber, peeled and cut into half-moons

Basil leaves, for garnish

Mung bean sprouts, for garnish

To prepare the sauce, finely grate the ginger on a ginger grater or fine grater to extract its juice (you should have about 1 tablespoon). Blend the ginger juice, peanuts, coconut, coconut water, almond butter, Braggs, garlic, turmeric, curry powder, and orange juice in a blender until smooth. Add the Thai chile to taste.

Place the cauliflower, carrot, cabbage, and cucumber in a bowl. Pour the sauce over the vegetables. Garnish with the basil and bean sprouts. Serve with Tom Yum (page 110), if desired.

Shangri La

The mystic land of the immortals is known in the Far East as Shangri La, and this dish will transport you there. This Asian-inspired dish is a delicious remedy for a stir-fry craving. When it was first invented, it was actually called "Stir-Free."

SERVES 4

¼ cup Bragg Liquid Aminos

1½ cups filtered water

Juice of 1 lemon

1 head broccoli, chopped

1 large carrot, shredded

½ small head napa cabbage, shredded

Seven-Star Sauce

3-inch piece fresh ginger

1 cup pine nuts, soaked 2 hours and drained

4 seeded, soaked dates (see page 42), drained

2 tablespoons raw tahini

2 tablespoons white miso

Filtered water as needed

¼ cup chopped green onions, for garnish

1 tablespoon black sesame seeds, for garnish

In a large bowl, combine the Braggs, water, and lemon juice. Add the broccoli, carrot, and cabbage. Let sit for 1 to 10 hours.

To prepare the sauce, finely grate the ginger on a ginger grater or fine grater to extract its juice (you should have about 2 tablespoons). In a blender, mix the ginger juice, pine nuts, dates, tahini, miso, and enough water to create a thick, creamy consistency.

Drain the marinated vegetables and transfer to a serving bowl. Pour the sauce over the vegetables, mix well, and garnish with green onions and black sesame seeds.

Nori Rolls

This was the most popular dish ever at The Raw Experience. We'd sometimes roll up to fifty nori rolls in a day. Nori can be rolled on a bamboo sushi mat or by hand. Once rolled, it takes skill to cut the nori. Be sure to use a wet, serrated knife and to keep the seam side down. Nori rolls can be sliced into 9, sometimes even 13 pieces. It takes skill and patience to master nori rolling and cutting, but once you figure it out it's a snap. Nori is very versatile and many different things can be rolled inside. Experiment with your own preferences of flavor and rolling.

SERVES 4

- 4 sheets nori (make certain they are dried, not toasted)
- 3 cups loosely packed field greens
- 1 cup Festive Seed Cheeze (page 145)
- 1 cup Carrot-Almond Pâté (page 140)
- 1 avocado, peeled, pitted, and sliced
- 1 carrot, cut into ⅛-inch-thick strips
- 1 beet, cut into ⅛-inch-thick strips
- 1 cup loosely packed sunflower sprouts (see page 44)
- ¼ cup sesame seeds, for garnish

For each roll place a nori sheet on a roller or the counter shiny side down with the ridges running vertically. Lay a few greens on the sheet 1 inch from one edge. Cover with ¼ cup of seed cheeze and ¼ cup of the pâté. Top with one-quarter of each of the avocado, carrot, beet, and sprouts. Fold the nori sheet in half and firmly envelop the contents by tucking the folded sheet edge underneath the contents. Roll the nori sheet into a cylinder, wrapping the contents firmly. Moisten the outside edge of the nori sheet and seal. Let sit, seam side down, for 2 minutes. Cut with a wet, serrated knife. Serve garnished with the sesame seeds.

Desserts

Carob Devastation

This recipe was a celebratory moment in the world of raw cuisine. I always told stories about a cake I loved called "chocolate devastation," from an upscale restaurant named Luma, in New York City. At the Raw Experience, we came up with this raw version of a carob cake. I dubbed it Carob Devastation in honor of my favorite cake, and it became a permanent feature on our menu.

SERVES 8 TO 10

1 cup sprouted almonds
  (see page 44)

2 cups seeded, soaked dates
  (see page 42), drained

1 cup soaked raisins (see
  page 42), drained

1 tablespoon pure vanilla
  extract

3 cups carrot pulp (from juicing
  carrots)

2 cups walnuts

2 cups sunflower seeds

1 cup fresh coconut, shredded

1 cup raw carob powder

2 cups Nut Crème (page 170)

In a food processor, grind the almonds, dates, raisins and vanilla. In a large bowl, mix the carrot pulp with the almond mixture. In a food processor, grind the walnuts and sunflower seeds into a fine powder. In a separate bowl, mix the powdered walnuts and sunflower seeds, the coconut, and carob. Gradually add the dry coconut mixture into the wet almond-carrot mixture, and stir well. On a serving plate, form into a cake shape and spread the nut crème over the top.

Raw Fruit Pies

No one is really certain who made the first raw fruit pie. I learned from Lenny Watson, Lenny learned from Victoras Kulvinskas, and who knows where Victoras found out about it—I haven't asked him yet. All I know is that it just keeps getting better. Our pies at the Raw Experience were "to live for" and many knew us as the folks who put the pie in Paia. These pie recipes below are really just guides. Be inspired and be creative and your talent will amaze you.

SERVES 8 (MAKES ONE 9-INCH PIE)

Carob Almond Crust

1 cup sprouted almonds (see page 44)

5 seeded, soaked dates (see page 42), drained

¼ teaspoon ground cinnamon

¼ teaspoon ground allspice

1 tablespoon raw carob powder

or

Walnut Zing Crust

1 cup sprouted walnuts (see page 44)

5 seeded, soaked dates (see page 42), drained

¼ teaspoon ground cinnamon

¼ teaspoon freshly grated lemon zest

or

Praline Crust

1 cup sprouted pecans (see page 44)

5 seeded, soaked dates (see page 42), drained

¼ teaspoon pure vanilla extract

¼ teaspoon nutmeg

or

Nut-Free Crust

1 cup dried banana pieces

5 seeded, soaked dates (see page 42), drained

½ cup soaked raisins (see page 42), drained

¼ teaspoon ground cinnamon

¼ teaspoon ground allspice

Oil, for greasing pan (optional)

Raw carob powder, for sprinkling

Nut Crème

5 dates, seeded

1 cup filtered water

1 cup soaked nuts (such as cashews, almonds, or hazelnuts; see page 42), drained

4 cups fresh fruit pieces (such as blueberries, papaya, banana, cherimoya, sapote, or shredded coconut)

½ cup berries, for garnish

1 papaya, peeled, seeded, and sliced, for garnish

To prepare any of the four crusts, place all of the ingredients in a food processor and pulse a few times to combine. Continue grinding until the mixture forms a thick paste. Oil or moisten with water a 9-inch pie plate and sprinkle with the carob powder to coat (the carob powder helps keep the pie crust from sticking to the plate). Form the crust mixture into a ball and press it from the center of the pie plate out toward the edges, spreading as evenly as possible. Set aside.

To prepare the nut crème, place the dates in a small bowl, cover with the water, and soak for about 1 hour, or until soft. Drain, reserving ¼ cup of the liquid. Place the dates, reserved liquid, and nuts in a blender or blender cup, and grind until smooth.

To prepare the fruit, you may slice the fruit, purée the fruit, leave it whole, or any combination of the three. Fill the pie crust with the prepared fruit. Top with the nut crème and garnish with the berries and papaya slices, arranged in a sunburst formation.

Coconut Custard

This smooth and creamy dessert is a Hawaiian specialty. In old Hawaii, it was a custom to plant five coconut trees for each child born. This was to provide all of the basic food, clothing, and shelter they would need. Today there is an abundance of coconuts in Hawaii, and this custard is a true "local kine" recipe.

SERVES 2 TO 4

3 dates, seeded
½ cup filtered water
2 cups young coconut meat
1 teaspoon pure vanilla extract

Place the dates in a small bowl, cover with the water, and soak for about 1 hour, or until soft. In a blender cup or small food processor, blend the dates along with their soaking water, the coconut, and the vanilla into a smooth custard. Spoon into individual bowls, cover, refrigerate until chilled, and serve.

Brownies

These brownies were one of the first raw desserts I attempted, thanks to my friend Sena, who taught me how to make them. Whenever I visited her house, she would always have these in the refrigerator waiting for me.

SERVES 8 TO 10

2 cups figs, soaked in water until soft and drained

2 cups seeded, soaked dates (see page 42), drained

2 cups sprouted almonds (see page 44)

½ cup raw carob powder

2 tablespoons pure vanilla extract

2 cups Nut Crème (page 170)

In a homogenizing juicer with the blank plate in place, homogenize the figs, dates, and almonds into a bowl. Add the carob powder and the vanilla and mix well. Form ¼ cup of the mixture into a 1-inch thick square and spread 2 tablespoons of the nut crème on top. Repeat for the remaining brownies. Refrigerate overnight before serving.

Lemon Bars

These easy snack bars dry quickly and have a tangy, sweet flavor.

SERVES 4

1 cup sprouted oats (see page 44)

1 cup soaked almonds (see page 42), drained

½ cup seeded, soaked dates (see page 42), drained

3 tablespoons freshly grated lemon zest

Juice of 1 lemon

Using a homogenizing juicer, homogenize the oats, almonds, and dates until smooth. Transfer the mixture to a large bowl and mix in the lemon zest and juice. Press evenly into an 18-inch dehydrator tray, ½ inch thick. Using one of the methods described on page 45, dehydrate the bars for 18 hours. Cut out of the tray into bars and dry longer. The bars shouldn't be super sticky. Refrigerate until chilled and serve.

Carob-Hazelnut Torte

When I was visiting San Francisco in 1995, I helped this crazy cat Juliano start a restaurant called RAW. Eventually, I bought RAW and turned it into the Raw Experience, but before then, when RAW was being born, one of the first things I noticed was Juliano had no desserts on the menu. I invented this torte and it became the first dessert served at RAW. Soon after, I was asked to print the recipes in the San Jose Mercury News. *I never did see the article, but I did get hundreds of calls about it from people who loved it. This rich and filling treat became a standard at the Raw Experience.*

SERVES 8 TO 12

2 cups seeded, soaked dates (see page 42), drained

3 cups soaked hazelnuts (see page 42), drained

1 cup raw carob powder

½ cup dried shredded coconut

2 tablespoons pure vanilla extract

2 cups Nut Crème (page 170)

1 cup Carob Sauce (page 177)

1 cup blackberries, for garnish

Mint leaves, for garnish

Using a homogenizing juicer, homogenize the dates and hazelnuts and place in a large bowl. Mix in the carob powder and coconut. Add the vanilla and stir. Using wet hands, roll the mixture into a ball. On a serving plate, press the ball into a flat circle, 1 inch thick. Top with nut crème and drizzle with carob sauce. Garnish with the blackberries and mint leaves.

Sesame Rawies

These sweet little rawies are quick and easy to make and have a great crunch when fully dried.

SERVES 4 TO 6

2 cups sprouted sesame seeds (see page 44)

1 cup sprouted sunflower seeds (see page 44)

1½ cups seeded, soaked dates (see page 42), drained

1 tablespoon pure vanilla extract

Using a homogenizing juicer, homogenize all of the ingredients until smooth and place in a large bowl. Form into ½-inch balls and place them on a drying tray. Using one of the methods described on page 45, dehydrate the balls for about 12 hours, or until firm.

Carrot Kake

This delicious dessert is as simple as can be. Carrot pulp (the part that is left when juice is removed) is a very versatile substance that is sweet, light, and easy to form. This recipe is a perfect way to make use of its many virtues.

SERVES 8 TO 12

Frosting

1½ cups soaked cashews (see page 44), drained

½ cup seeded, soaked dates (see page 42), drained

¼ cup freshly squeezed lemon juice

1 tablespoon pure vanilla extract

3 cups sprouted almonds (see page 44)

2 cups seeded, soaked dates (see page 42), drained

2 cups soaked raisins (see page 42), drained

6 cups carrot pulp (from juicing carrots)

1 tablespoon freshly grated lemon zest

1 tablespoon freshly grated orange zest

1 tablespoon ground cinnamon

½ tablespoon ground nutmeg

1 tablespoon ground cardamom

To prepare the frosting, place the cashews, dates, lemon juice, and vanilla in a blender and blend until smooth. Set aside.

To prepare the kake, using a homogenizing juicer, homogenize the almonds, dates, and raisins. In a large bowl, combine the almond mixture and the carrot pulp. Add the lemon zest, orange zest, cinnamon, nutmeg, and cardamom. Mix well. On a serving plate, form into a cake shape and top with the frosting. Refrigerate until chilled before serving.

Bliss Balls

These fantastic little treats are one of the oldest recipes I know. As a child, I learned to make nut-butter refrigerator balls. These Bliss Balls are the raw evolution of my mother's recipe. Many people tell me of the blissful experience they get from eating this most delectable of desserts.

SERVES 4 TO 6

1 cup sprouted oats (see page 44) or Buckies (see page 176)

1 cup seeded, soaked dates (see page 42), drained

1 cup raw nut butter (such as almond or hazelnut)

1/2 cup soaked raisins (see page 42), drained

1 teaspoon pure vanilla extract

1/4 cup raw carob powder

1 tablespoon ground cinnamon

1 cup raw wheat germ or sunflower seeds, ground into a fine powder (if needed to dry out mix)

1 cup sesame seeds

In a food processor, mix the oats, dates, nut butter, raisins, vanilla, carob, and cinnamon. Add the wheat germ only if the oat mixture is runny. The oak mixture should be tacky, like cookie dough. Spread the sesame seeds on a tray or plate. Roll the oat mixture into 1- to 2-inch balls, then roll the balls in the sesame seeds to coat. Serve.

Frozen Fudge

This fudge is sweet and semiaddictive. Many of my students love this recipe and make it a daily staple in their homes. This stuff tastes so good and melts in your mouth—just be careful not to eat too much!

SERVES 6 TO 10

1 cup dates, seeded

1½ cups filtered water

1 tablespoon pure vanilla extract

1½ cups nut butter (such as almond or hazelnut)

1½ cups raw carob powder

½ cup dried shredded coconut

Place the dates in a bowl, cover with the water, and soak for about 1 hour, or until soft. Drain, reserving the liquid. In a blender, blend the dates and vanilla until smooth, slowly adding soaking water as needed to form a creamy consistency. Transfer the date mixture into a large bowl, add the nut butter, and stir to combine. In a separate bowl, mix the carob and coconut. Gradually add the dry carob mixture into the wet date mixture. Stir well. Press evenly into a 10 by 18-inch brownie pan, 1 inch thick, and freeze until firm, about 3 hours. To serve, cut into 1-inch squares.

Buckies

This recipe is one of the greatest ever invented. Buckies are a sprouted buckwheat snack treat, cereal, salad topping, and more. Their nutritional value is very high and the taste is delectable. This is possibly the crunchiest treat in the world of raw foods.

SERVES 4

2 cups dates

2 cups filtered water

1 teaspoon pure vanilla extract

4 cups sprouted buckwheat (see page 44), well drained

Place the dates in a bowl, cover with the water, and soak for about 1 hour, or until soft. Drain, reserving ½ cup of the liquid. In a blender, combine the dates, reserved liquid, and vanilla. Pour the date mixture into a large bowl and add the buckwheat sprouts. Mix well. Using one of the methods described on page 45, spread the mixture ½ inch thick on the appropriate drying surface and dehydrate the buckies for 7 to 10 hours. Crumble apart and use as a topping or just eat as a snack.

Six-Layer Carob Kake

This fabulous cake was originally created for a wedding. These cakes can turn out beautifully if you decorate and garnish them well, so be artistic.

SERVES 10 TO 12

6 bananas

2 cups seeded, soaked dates (see page 42), drained

½ cup raw wheat germ

2 cups raw carob powder

1 cup sprouted walnuts (see page 44)

Carob Sauce

4 seeded, soaked dates (see page 42), drained

¼ cup raw carob powder

2 tablespoons olive oil

3 cups Nut Crème (page 170)

Using a homogenizing juicer, homogenize the bananas, dates, wheat germ, carob, and walnuts into a bowl. Divide the dough into six equal-sized balls and form six round, flat layers of similar width and diameter. Using one of the methods described on page 45, dehydrate the dough for 12 hours, or until dry.

To prepare the sauce, place the dates, carob powder, and olive oil in a blender cup or blender, and blend well.

To assemble the cake, place one of the six layers on a plate. Spread ½ cup of the nut crème over the layer. Continue layering, alternating cake and frosting, with the next five cake layers. Generously frost the top and sides of the cake. Drizzle with the carob sauce and serve.

Banana Bread

Bananas are actually an herb plant, not a fruit, and we eat its flowering stalk. There are hundreds of varieties of bananas and they grow wild all over Maui. A banana tree can grow from seed to fruit in just nine months. These prolific trees provide an excellent source of nourishment and energy. This is true gorilla food.

SERVES 4

½ cup seeded, soaked dates (see page 42), drained

4 to 6 bananas, peeled and thickly sliced (about 4 cups)

1 cup raw wheat germ

1 cup sprouted oats or buckwheat (see page 44)

In a food processor, blend all of the ingredients until well combined but chunky. Form the mixture into small patties and place on a dehydrator sheet. Using one of the methods described on page 45, dehydrate for 18 hours, flipping at least once during drying time.

Apple Kake

This ultimately healthy cake is a light and spicy dessert that lets you have your cake and eat it, too.

SERVES 4 TO 6

1 cup flax seeds

½-inch piece fresh ginger

1 cup sprouted oats (see page 44)

1 cup seeded, soaked dates (see page 42), drained

1 teaspoon ground cinnamon, plus additional for garnish

1 teaspoon ground nutmeg

1 tablespoon freshly grated lemon zest

2 apples, shredded (about 1½ cups)

Nut Crème (page 170, optional)

In a spice grinder or blender cup, grind the flax seeds into a fine powder. Finely grate the ginger on a ginger grater or fine grater to extract its juice (you should have about 1 teaspoon). In a food processor, process the flax seed powder, ginger juice, oats, dates, the 1 teaspoon cinnamon, the nutmeg, and lemon zest until smooth. Transfer to a bowl and fold in the shredded apples. Form the mixture into a cake shape, 4 inches thick and 9 inches in diameter. Frost with the nut crème and, using one of the methods described on page 45, dehydrate the cake for 4 to 6 hours. Sprinkle cinnamon on top and allow to set in the refrigerator about 2 hours.

Oat-Date Rawies

It's great to be able to make quick and tasty desserts. These simple treats keep well and are fabulous to break out when unexpected company stops in for a rawie and a glass of nut mylk.

SERVES 4 TO 6

2 cups sprouted oats (see page 44)

1 cup seeded, soaked dates (see page 42), drained

1 cup soaked raisins (see page 42), drained

1 tablespoon ground cinnamon

Using a homogenizing juicer, homogenize the oats and dates until smooth and place in a large bowl. Stir in the raisins and cinnamon. For each rawie, form 2 tablespoons of the dough into a ball, place on a drying tray, and press into a ½-inch round. Repeat for the remaining rawies. Using one of the methods described on page 45, dehydrate the rawies for 18 hours, or until dry.

Ultimate Sundae

Something similar to this great dessert recipe came with my Champion Juicer. It is nice to know that the people who make that very versatile juicer enjoy the simplicity of raw-food ice cream. This dessert is a true winner.

SERVES 2 TO 4

6 bananas, peeled, frozen, and thickly sliced

11 strawberries, frozen

2 cups fresh coconut meat

2 cups Cashew Sauce (recipe follows) or Carob Sauce (page 177)

Berries or crushed walnuts, for garnish

Using a homogenizing juicer with the blank plate in place, homogenize the bananas, strawberries, and coconut separately. Transfer equal amounts of each homogenized fruit to individual bowls. Stir the homogenized fruits in each bowl until swirled. Top each with some of the cashew sauce and berries, or carob sauce and crushed walnuts. Serve immediately.

Cashew Sauce

This fabulous sauce is a smoother version of our standard nut crème. Use this one on any dessert or just dip Fruit Rawies (page 50) in it.

MAKES 2 CUPS

1 cup soaked cashews (see page 42), drained

4 seeded, soaked dates (see page 42), drained

1 teaspoon pure vanilla extract

¼ cup filtered water

Combine all of the ingredients in a food processor or blender and blend until smooth.

Reading List

These are a few books about or relating to raw foods. Some of the titles are out of print, but you may be able to special order them via booksellers or find them in used-book stores.

Books by Viktoras Kulvinskas:
Survival into the Twenty-First Century
Love Your Body
Sprout for the Love of Every Body

Books by Dr. Ann Wigmore:
Be Your Own Doctor
The Wheatgrass Book
The Sprouting Book
The Healing Power Within
Recipes for a Longer Life
Naturama

Books by Bernard Jenson:
The Real Soup and Salad Book
Blending Magic
The Healing Power of Chlorophyll

Sweet Temptations
by Frances Kendall

The LifeFood Recipe Book
by Annie and David Jubb

Dry It—You'll Like It
by Gen MacManiman

Wheatgrass Juice: Gift of Nature
by Betsy Russell Manning

Books by Steve "the Sproutman" Meyrowitz:
Sproutman's Kitchen Garden Cookbook
Recipes from the Sproutman
Wheatgrass: Nature's Finest Medicine

Books by Edmond Bordeaux Szekely:
Essene Gospel of Peace
Scientific Vegetarianism
The Book of Living Foods
The Ecological Health Garden

Dining in the Raw
by Rita Romano

*The Garden of Eden Raw Fruit and
    Vegetable Recipes*
by Phyllis Avery

Digestion, Assimilation, Elimination, and You
by Ed Bashaw and Michael Diogo

Raw Fruits and Vegetable Book
by Max E. Bircher, M.D., and
    M. Bircher-Benner, M.D.

Fruitarianism and Physical Rejuvenation
by O. L. M. Abramowski, M.D.

Live Food Juices
by H. E. Kirshner

Regenerative Diet
by Dr. John R. Christopher, N.D., M.H.

Books by Paul Braggs:
South Sea Culture of the Abdomen
Salt Free Health Sauerkraut Cookbook

Blatant Raw Foodist Propaganda
by Joe Alexander

The Exotic Fruit Book
by Norman Van Aken

Vibrant Living
by James Levin, M.D., and
    Natalie Cederquist

*Juel Anderson's Sea Green Primer:
    A Beginner's Book of Seaweed Cookery*
by Juel Anderson

The Original Diet
by Karen Cross Whyte

Sprouts
by Esther Munroe

How to Dry Fruit
by Deanna DeLong

Warming Up to Living Foods
by Elysa Markowitz

Index